KW-053-358

Contents

America ...

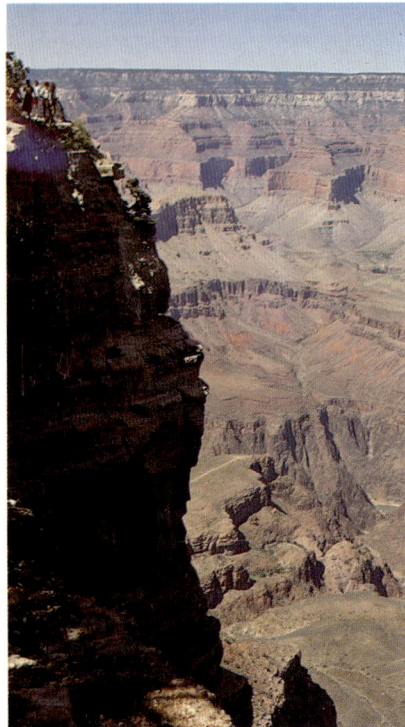

America – the very name sets the imagination going non-stop. The Wild West, the Grand Canyon, the Golden Gate, Niagara Falls, Disneyland, the White House – a hundred images flash across the mind at the thought of this vast land. Unforgettable sights and experiences such as the bright lights of Las Vegas and Hollywood, the natural wonders of Monument Valley and the Rocky Mountains, the bustling, exciting cities of New York and New Orleans and the wide-open spaces of the prairies and Alaska.

All these places are in the United States of America (USA). This is the country that most people call America. The Rocky Mountains, the prairies and Niagara Falls are also in Canada. The USA and Canada are the two biggest countries in the vast continent of North America. Together, they cover an area of 20 million km^2 – over 80 times the area of Great Britain. This book is about these two huge countries.

> The first thing a foreigner has to try to take in about America – and it is not something automatically grasped even by the natives – is simply the size of the place .... (Alistair Cooke, *America*, BBC, 1973)

NORTH AMERICA

Michael Shorthouse

21123828R

TS

CENTRAL REGIONAL LIBRARY SERVICE

21123828R

GEOGRAPHY 10-14

Macdonald

F

A MACDONALD BOOK

© Macdonald & Co (Publishers) Ltd 1986

First published in Great Britain in 1986 by
Macdonald & Co (Publishers) Ltd
London & Sydney

A BPCC plc company

All rights reserved

Printed in the Netherlands by
Imago Publishing

Macdonald & Co (Publishers) Ltd
Greater London House
Hampstead Road
London NW1 7QX

British Library Cataloguing in Publication Data
Shorthouse, Michael
    North America.—(Geography 10-14; 11)
    1. North America—Description and travel—1981-
    I. Title   II. Series
    917   E41
    ISBN 0-356-11390-6

Acknowledgements

The publishers thank the following for permission to reproduce their photographs and other copyright materials. The numbers refer to pages and L, R, T, B indicate left, right, top and bottom respectively.

Barnaby's Picture Library 14, 25; Bettmann Archive/BBC Hulton Picture Library 11; BPCC/Aldus Archive 6B, 12, 18 (Denver Public Library); Camera Press 40, 47; Sally and Richard Greenhill 6T, 9B, 34, 35, 38; Greyhound Lines 42B; Robert Harding Picture Library 9TR, 10, 27L & R. 41; The Image Bank 24T (Jeff Smith), 29 (Harald Suno), 32 (Gregory Heisler); Eric Inglefield 4BL; John Massey-Stewart 33; Peter Newark's Western Americana 15, 19; Popperfoto 42T; Rex Features 17B, 23, 26L; Mike Shorthouse 13BL, 45T & B; Spectrum 9T & C, 37T; Frank Spooner Pictures 21, 26TR, 37B; Vautier de-Nanxe Picture Library, Paris 13T, 22, 24B, 31; ZEFA 4TL & TR, 13BR, 17T, 20; Parks Canada 45.

Cover photograph: Frank Spooner/Gamma

The artwork illustrations are by Swanston Graphics

GEOGRAPHY 10-14

Series Editor: Richard Kemp
Buckinghamshire County Adviser in Humanities
Formerly Head of Humanities Faculty,
Lord Williams's School, Thame

North America

Editor: John Day
Designer: Swanston Graphics
Picture Research: Suzanne Williams
Production: Ken Holt

Series Consultants:
Barbara Hamnett, Head of Geography,
J.F.S. Comprehensive School, Camden
David Robinson, Headmaster, Blue Coat School, Dudley
Michael Storm, Staff Inspector of Geography, Inner London Education Authority
Michael Weller, Co-ordinator of PGCE Programme Bulmershe College of Higher Education, Reading
David Wright, Lecturer in Education, University of East Anglia, Norwich

Editorial note

Economic division of the world
Throughout this series the terms **North** and **South** are used to divide the world into its two major areas of different economic characteristics. This is in accord with the model proposed in the *Brandt Report*, which is becoming widely adopted. North and South can be broadly equated with the wealthy, technologically advanced countries and the poorer, less technologically advanced countries respectively. They replace such terms as 'developed countries' and 'developing', 'less developed', or 'underdeveloped countries' or Third World – all of which, for a number of reasons, are less than satisfactory. The term North derives from the fact that the countries in this category, with the exception of Australia and New Zealand, lie in the northern hemisphere and north of the tropics.

Glossary
Terms which readers may be meeting for the first time or which have a special meaning in the context of this book are listed in the glossary on page 48. The first time such a term appears it is printed in **bold type** (except in the case of illustrations). Other appropriate terms are also included.

Copy No. 1

Class No. J917

Author SHO

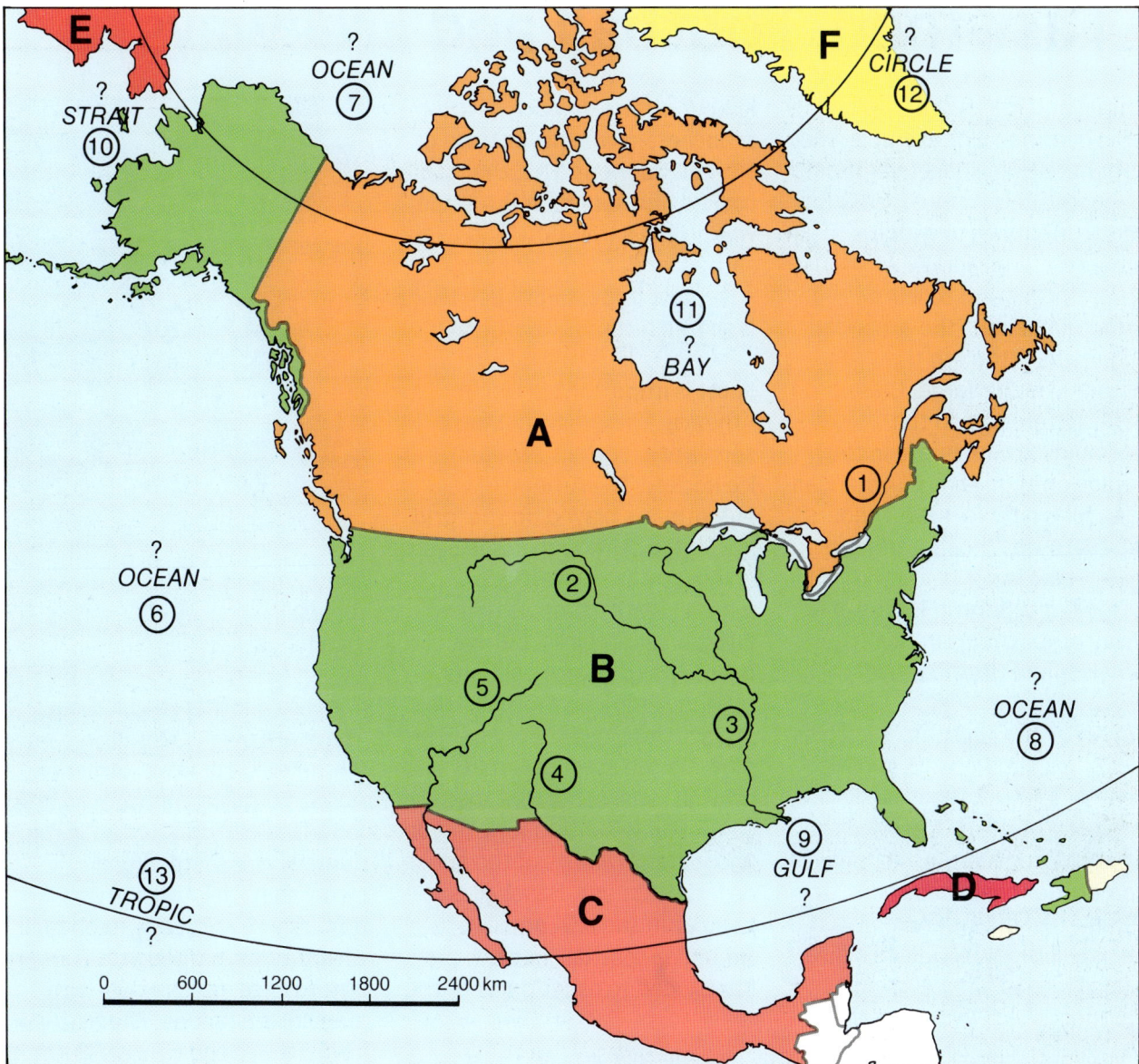

Map labels:
- E
- ? OCEAN (7)
- F
- ? CIRCLE (12)
- ? STRAIT (10)
- (11) ? BAY
- A
- (1)
- ? OCEAN (6)
- (2)
- B
- (5)
- (3)
- ? OCEAN (8)
- (4)
- (9) GULF ?
- D
- (13) TROPIC ?
- C

Scale: 0 600 1200 1800 2400 km

1 What does America make you think about? Perhaps it is something mentioned on these pages, or a favourite TV programme, or sport, or food. Write down one thing, describe it and say why you think it is so 'American'.

2 The photographs on page 4 show well-known sights in North America. Try to name them and find out where they are. Choose one of the pictures and write about it. (You may use other books to help you.)

3 Copy the map above. With the help of your atlas, name the following in a 'key' by the side of your map:
(a) countries A to F
(b) rivers 1 to 5
(c) the oceans, gulf, strait and bay numbered 6 to 11
(d) the lines of latitude numbered 12 and 13

4 On your map, mark the locations of the sights shown in the photographs.

5 Use the scale on your map to

Above North America and neighbouring countries.

work out the distance from New York to San Francisco and from northern Alaska to southern Florida.

6 **Project idea:** Imagine you are writing the introduction to a holiday brochure describing trips to North America. What would you choose to attract holidaymakers? Plan out an imaginary page, including pictures or drawings if you wish.

Fast-food, Football and Freeways

Britain and North America have a lot in common. For example, they both have English as their main language. This makes it easy for people in Britain to watch American films and TV programmes and so learn something about the American way of life. Although the language is the same, there are many differences in the meanings of words and in the names given to things. American cars, for example, have 'fenders', 'mufflers' and 'hoods' and run on 'gas'. This idea of being the 'same but different' is true of many other things in North America and Britain.

Big American companies such as Coca-Cola and Pepsi-Cola have done much to spread the influence of the USA around the world. More recently, McDonald's hamburger chain has been established in Britain. Known by its big 'M' sign, McDonald's gives a good idea of what is meant by 'fast-foods'. In North America, McDonald's and dozens of other companies, such as Burger King, Big Boy, Pizza Hut and Kentucky Fried Chicken, all offer a similar kind of service. In each of their branches, in whichever town or city you happen to be, the food is cooked and served in the same way, in the same time and to the same standard. Quality and speed are important when there is so much competition.

Sport is important in North America. The main spectator sports are football, baseball and ice hockey. The American version of football is played on the 'grid-iron' pitch. Although some soccer and rugby are played, it is football teams such as the Pittsburgh Steelers, Denver Broncos and Miami Dolphins, playing American football, that attract the biggest crowds. They play in huge stadiums that provide family entertainment, comfortable seating for everyone and instant replays of the action on large screens. Baseball is very popular in the USA and, like American football, has been introduced to other parts of the

1 A fast-food cafeteria.

world, mainly by the US armed forces. Ice hockey is Canada's leading game.

Cars are another major thing. There are over 100 million cars on the roads of North America. About 16 million of them can be found in California, which is the number one state for car ownership. Los Angeles was probably the first city to be built with the car in mind. It has many freeways, or motorways, with huge interchanges. The freeways have a top speed limit of 88 km/h. In spite of this, about 50 000 people die in traffic accidents in the USA every year.

2 An interchange on a Los Angeles freeway at night. It is estimated that almost a third of the land area of Los Angeles is taken up by freeways, roads, garages, petrol stations, car parks and other things needed for cars.

The National Football League

Atlanta Falcons	Miami Dolphins
Buffalo Bills	Minnesota Vikings
Chicago Bears	(Minneapolis)
Cincinnati Bengals	New England Patriots
Cleveland Browns	(Boston)
Dallas Cowboys	New Orleans Saints
Denver Broncos	New York Giants
Detroit Lions	New York Jets
Green Bay Packers	Philadelphia Eagles
(Green Bay and	Pittsburgh Steelers
Milwaukee)	St Louis Cardinals
Houston Oilers	San Diego Chargers
Indianapolis Colts	San Francisco 49ers
Kansas City Chiefs	Seattle Seahawks
Los Angeles Raiders	Tampa Bay Buccaneers
Los Angeles Rams	Washington Redskins

Prince Rupert Dawson Creek 6 8½ Edmonton 11 11 Prince George 13 18 3½ 21 Winnipeg Quebec 3 St Stephen Calgary 18 Montreal 8 10½ Vancouver 12 18½ 25 Sudbury 5½ 10 7 8 5½ 3½ Boston Seattle 4 7 Spokane Duluth Toronto 6 Albany 3½ 4½ Portland 4 9 14½ Billings 14 Fargo 3 11 19 Detroit Buffalo 5 4 4½ 9½ 7½ New York 24 5½ Minneapolis 8 Milwaukee 2 6 3½ Cleveland 6½ 2 4½ Philadelphia 22 11 10 Chicago 7½ Columbus 3 3½ Pittsburgh 5 Washington Cheyenne 12 Omaha 4 6½ 6 12½ Salt Lake City 10 11½ 5 Indianapolis 2½ Cincinnati Richmond 2 Norfolk 14 16 2½ Kansas City St Louis 4½ 2½ 2½ 16 Denver 11½ 15 5 7 8 Louisville 8½ Knoxville 7 3 Reno 12 6 10 8 Nashville 3½ 5½ 2½ Charlotte 13½ Raleigh Sacramento 3 11½ Oklahoma City 2½ Tulsa Chattanooga 4 4 5 12 San Francisco 2 12 10 Las Vegas 11 12 Memphis 6 Birmingham 3½ Atlanta 9 27 Albuquerque 6 Amarillo Dallas 10 9 7½ 14 17 Jacksonville 6 8 20 16 7 12 Tallahassee 7½ Los Angeles 11 8½ 20 11 10 16 Mobile 9 7 6½ 8½ 2½ 9 9 Phoenix 14 7 New Orleans 4 7 14 San Diego 10 2½ 9½ Tucson 7 12 6 4 Houston 8 St Petersburg 7 7½ Miami El Paso San Antonio 3 Laredo

N

1 (a) Write down the following American names for things: fender, muffler, hood, gas, trash-can, elevator, sidewalk, drug-store, liquor store, parking lot, cookies, candies. Now try to work out what these things are called in Britain.
(b) List any other American words you can think of. Opposite each one write down the word used in Britain.

2 (a) What types of food would you expect to be able to buy as 'fast-food'?
(b) Why do you think fast-foods are so popular?

3 There are 28 teams in the National Football League (NFL) of the USA (see the box on page 6).
(a) With the help of your atlas, correctly position them on your own copy of a map of the USA.
(b) Compare your finished map with a map showing population density (see page 27). What do you notice?
(c) Suggest reasons for what you have found.

4 Los Angeles has about 3.5 million cars and almost 3 million people.
(a) Why do you think there are so many cars?
(b) In what ways has Los Angeles tried to cope with so many cars?
(c) What sorts of problems are likely to face the city?

5 You are planning a Greyhound bus tour around North America, lasting several weeks. You will visit all the following places:

3 The approximate travelling times in hours taken by Greyhound buses between the main North American cities.

Chicago, Dallas, Dawson Creek, Denver, Las Vegas, Los Angeles, Miami, Montreal, Nashville, Salt Lake City, San Francisco, Vancouver and Washington DC.

You intend to start and end your trip in New York and wish to spend as little time as possible on the bus.
(a) Use picture 3, and write down the order in which you will visit the places listed above and the time it will take.
(b) Add up the total time your tour will take. Compare it with the time taken by other people in your group and see who has planned the quickest route.

The North American Landscape

When you think of the scenery of North America, what picture comes to your mind? The beaches and surf of California? The snowy peaks of the Rocky Mountains? The swamps of the Florida Everglades? North America has all these landscapes – and much, much more besides.

On the mountain slopes of the Sierra Nevada, in California, where it is warm and wet for much of the year, grow the tallest trees in the world. The Sequoia redwoods here reach 90 m high – about ten times taller than a house and as high as a tall block of flats. Yet only a few hundred kilometres from the Sierra Nevada there are no trees at all – only short, wiry grasses, cacti and other drought-resistant plants. This is the desert region of the south-west, where little rain falls. Death Valley is in this region.

There are other places, too, where plants have to overcome very harsh conditions. In the **tundra** region of the far north the summers are short, and the ground not far below the surface stays frozen all year. This is called permafrost.

Between the deserts of the south-west and the tundra of the north there is a great variety of scenery and natural vegetation. Huge areas of forest once covered North America. There were deciduous woodlands of birch, maple, oak and many other trees in the east, and coniferous forests of pine, fir and spruce further north and in the high mountains.

In the middle of North America, between the towering Rocky Mountains and the great Mississippi River, stretch the prairies. Until the Europeans arrived, the prairies were a 'sea of waving grass'. Millions of buffalo wandered in great herds across the rolling grasslands. The Europeans called these the Great Plains. They realized that this vast region was good farmland, and so they moved in.

With the arrival of the white settlers on the Great Plains, the Indians who lived and hunted there were pushed out and, in the end, forced to live in **reservations**. Nearly all the buffalo were killed. Today, most of the area is cultivated, with farms growing wheat, maize and many other crops. The Great Plains are now among the most productive areas of farmland in the world.

So, whatever picture of North America you might have had in your mind is probably true – but only for one part of this huge continent. For North America is a land of many contrasts.

1 Types of natural vegetation in North America.

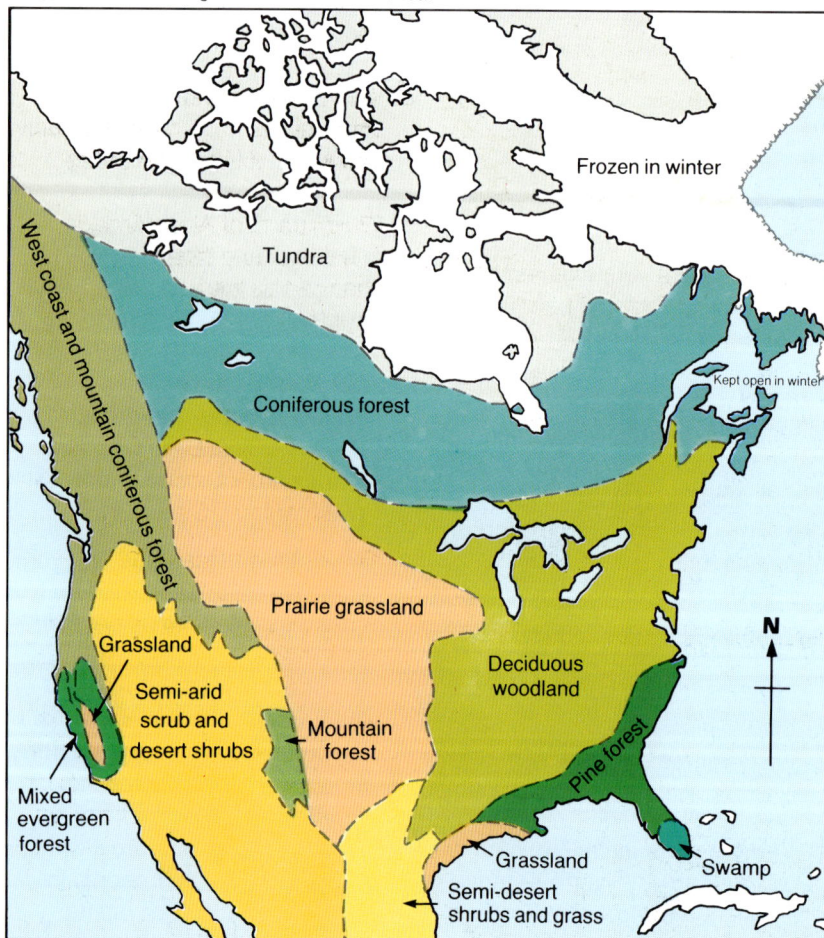

West coast and mountain coniferous forest

Frozen in winter

Tundra

Coniferous forest

Kept open in winter

Prairie grassland

Grassland

Semi-arid scrub and desert shrubs

Mountain forest

Deciduous woodland

N

Mixed evergreen forest

Pine forest

Grassland

Swamp

Semi-desert shrubs and grass

2 (above) The Athabaska Glacier.

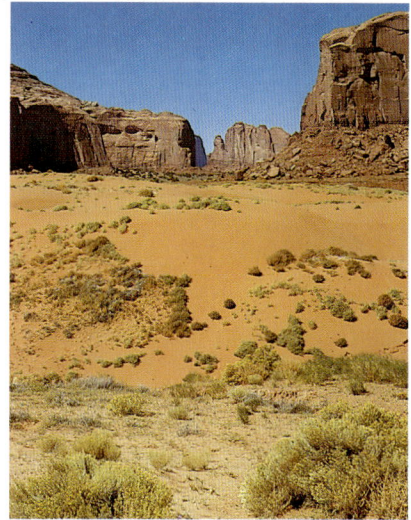

3 The desert region of the south-west.

4 (above) Forests and peaks of the Rocky Mountains.

5 (below) Grasslands of the Great Plains– the prairies.

1 Look at pictures 2 to 5.
(a) In which area would you most like to live? Why?
(b) In which area would you least like to live? Why?
(c) Which area would you choose for a holiday? Why?

2 Why have the prairies been changed perhaps more than any other part of North America?

3 Which parts of North America do you think have been least changed by the acitivties of people? Why?

4 Find a physical map of North America in your atlas.
(a) On an outline map of North America, mark on and name the following:

Rocky Mountains, Sierra Nevada, Appalachian Mountains; Central Lowlands; the Mississippi, Missouri, Ohio, Colorado and St Lawrence rivers; the Great Lakes (Lakes Superior, Michigan, Huron, Erie and Ontario); the Gulf of Mexico, Hudson Bay, Pacific Ocean and Atlantic Ocean.

(b) Use the numbers 1 to 4 to mark on the places shown in the pictures.

People in the Landscape

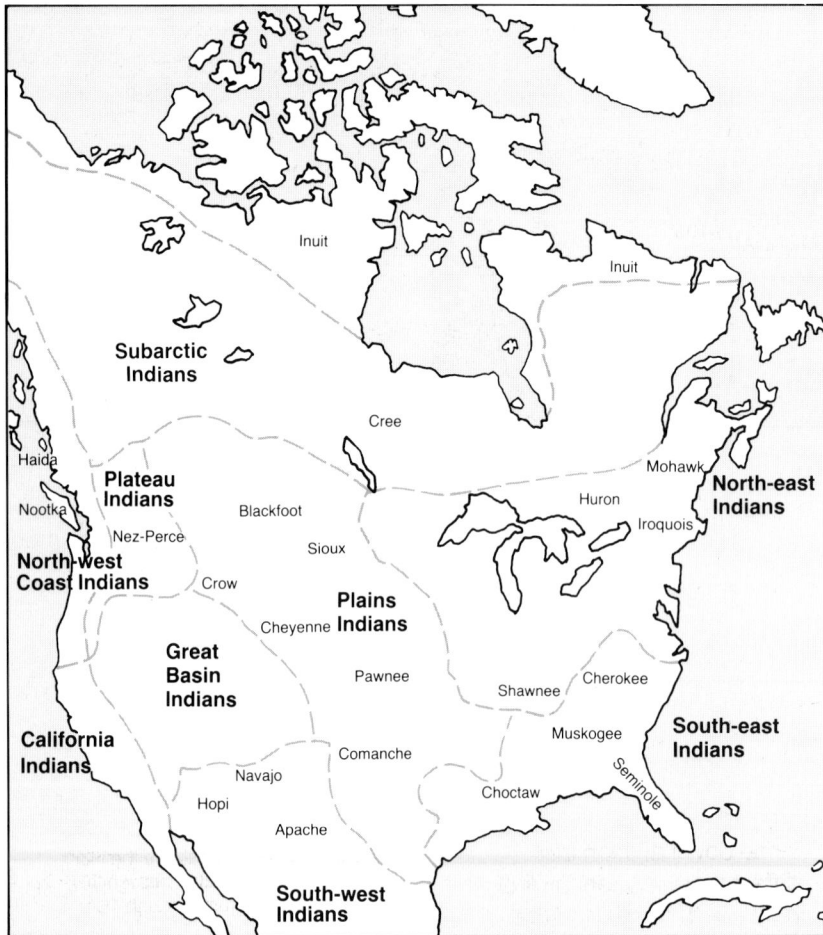

1 The main groups of Indians living in North America when the whites first arrived. Some of the main tribes within each group are also named.

thousands of years before the European settlers arrived and completely changed their ways of life. In the 1500s, before the main European take-over began, the native peoples numbered between five and ten million. Their many different ways of life were the result of their close relationship with their natural surroundings.

The Indians, as the Europeans called them, were split into several hundred tribes. These varied in size from many thousands of members to only a few dozen. Most had their own language or dialect and were divided into smaller groups called 'clans' and 'societies'. As in many parts of the world, people spent much time fighting each other. In North America, such tribal wars were common, with rivals being taken as slaves. The Indians were particularly skilled in the use of spears, clubs and bows and arrows. These were

The 5 km gap between Little Diomede Island (USA) and Big Diomede Island (USSR) separates more than just the continents of America and Asia. It is the dividing line between very different ways of life. The world's two great military superpowers face each other here across the 100 km of the Bering Strait. They are enemies in a 'cold war' that has resulted in the build-up of nuclear weapons by both sides since the early 1950s.

It is thus strange to think that the earliest peoples to live in

North America probably crossed what is now the Bering Strait to reach present-day Alaska. Some scientists believe that they arrived between 15 000 and 30 000 years ago. The sea-level may have been much lower then and they simply walked across on dry land. Other people suggest that they found their way over the ice sheets that covered the northern lands until about 10 000 years ago. They may even have used rafts or boats.

However they came, they were living in North America for

2 Weaving beautiful rugs is one of the many handicrafts still practised by the Navajo Indians of the south-west.

used both for fighting and hunting.

Films and TV may give the impression that horses have always played an important part in Indian life, but this is not so. Horses were first brought into North America by the Spanish settlers. It was not until the 1600s that the Plains Indians began to use horses to hunt buffalo.

The arrival of the Europeans was generally disastrous for the Indian tribes. New diseases brought by the Europeans killed thousands of them. The Indians were forced further and further west in a series of wars that lasted for over 300 years. They were then moved to reservations in areas that the new white settlers did not want. Since 1900 the original peoples of North America have numbered less than a million.

3 The Apache chief Geronimo led many attacks against the white settlers in Arizona during the 1880s.

1 Write down all the main differences you can think of between the USA and the USSR.

2 (a) Copy picture 4. Then work out and fill in the missing times and days.
(b) What will the times be in London, England?
(c) The International Date Line generally follows the 180° line of longitude. Why do you think it leaves this line for part of its route?
(d) What problems might there be if it did not change its course slightly?

3 Imagine you were a hunter living in eastern Siberia thousands of years ago. What might have caused you to leave your home and move to new and unknown lands?

4 The earth seen from above the North Pole. As the earth rotates through 360° in 24 h, it takes 1 h to turn through 15°.

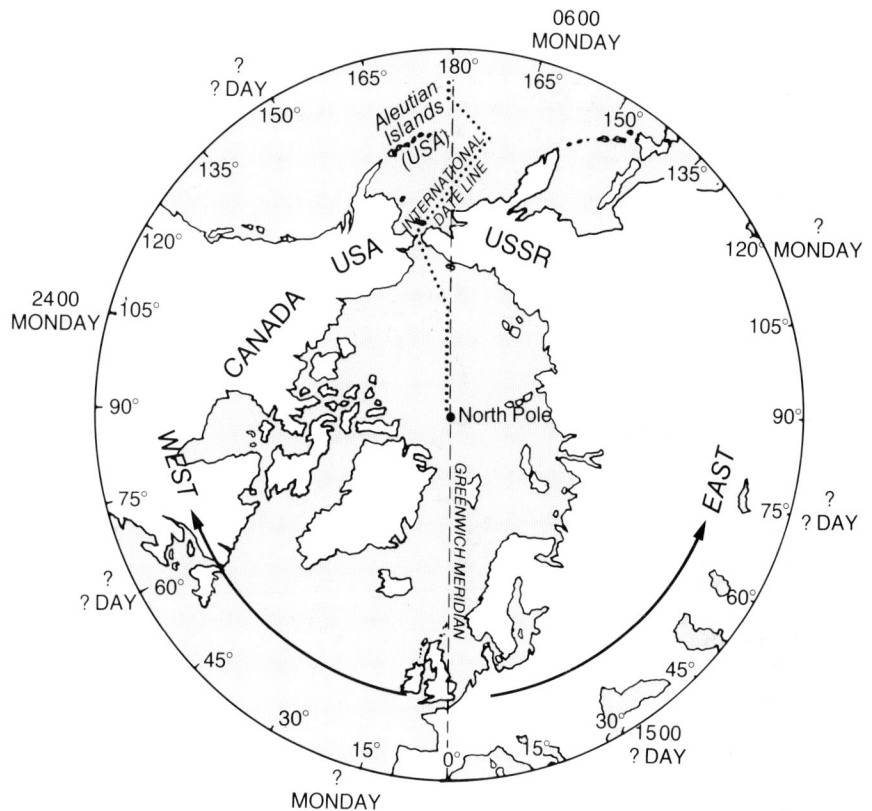

4 Why do you think that the Indians used a kind of sign language when they met people from other tribes?

5 What reasons can you suggest for the tribal wars?

6 Why did the Indians not use horses before the arrival of the Spaniards?

7 Project idea: Find out more about Indian reservations. Then describe how you think you would have felt if you had been forced to leave your home and made to live in a reservation somewhere else.

Living off the Land

1 A buffalo hunt on the Great Plains. The Indians of this region depended greatly on the buffalo for their food, and used the hides for clothing and shelter. They suffered greatly when white settlers, railway companies and then sportsmen arrived and shot the buffalo.

The Plains Indians were mostly nomadic. Herds of buffalo provided most of their needs. They killed only as many as they needed for their food, clothes and homes. Generally, a group of 300 to 500 led by a chief lived together in buffalo-hide **tipis** that could be taken down and folded easily.

The original peoples of North America lived in many different ways, depending on their natural surroundings. Their food, clothes, homes and also their art were all influenced by their **environment**.

In the treeless tundra of the far north lived groups of people often called Eskimos, who included the Inuit, Yupik and Inupiat. They arrived after the Indians and chose to live in small bands close to the coast. They hunted seals, whales and caribou. The northern coniferous forests became the home of the Cree Indians. They had no crops that would ripen in the short growing season, so they too depended on hunting and fishing.

The north-eastern Indians lived in woodlands of mostly deciduous trees, which gave them all they needed. They hunted, fished and collected fruits and roots. Some grew corn, beans and other vegetables in cleared patches. They used birch bark for canoes and sledges and for covering their dome-shaped huts. Some tribes were **nomadic**. Others lived in villages, which were often surrounded by high fences, or palisades, of pointed logs.

The south-eastern Indians had a similar way of life. Milder winters gave them a longer growing season and made farming easier. With better farming methods and the production of more food, the Indian population was able to grow larger in this region. Large settlements developed. Often the buildings were made from reeds and grass covered with mud.

In the desert regions of the south-west the Indians survived by hunting the scarce desert animals and digging up roots. It seems that, until about 700 years ago, there was enough rain for them to grow crops. These early farmers built stone villages into the sides of rocky canyons for protection. After the climate changed, nomadic groups, such as the Navajo, took up sheep-rearing.

Along the Pacific coast, the Indians of the drier southern areas gathered seeds, berries and nuts, and ground flour from acorns. The north-west coast Indians led a very different life. With plenty of animals to hunt, rivers filled with salmon and thick forests for timber, they lived well. They built large plank houses and carved and painted **totem poles**.

Native people	Main type of natural vegetation	Way of life	Use of local resources
Eskimos	Tundra	Hunted seals, whales and caribou	Homes and clothes from skins. Meat from animals. Heat and light from whale oil
Subarctic Indians	Coniferous forest	?	?

2 The way of life of the original native peoples of North America. See question 1.

3 (above) A buffalo-hide tipi of the Plains Indians.

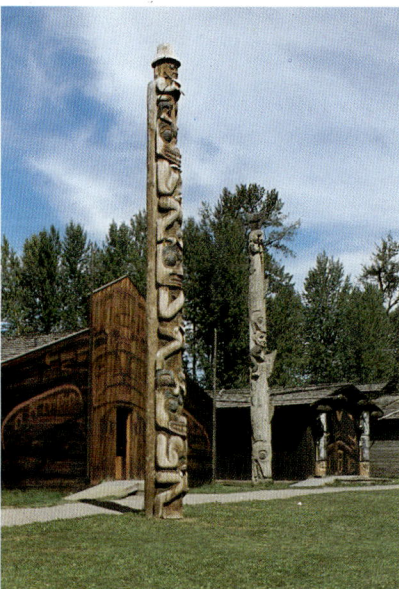

4 (left) Plank houses and totem poles of the north-west coast Indians.

5 (below) Houses of sun-baked mud, or 'adobe', built by Pueblo Indians of the south-west.

1 (a) Copy picture 1 on page 8.
(b) Make a tracing overlay of picture 1 on page 10.
(c) Copy out a table like the one shown left to list all the main groups of native North American peoples. Use your two maps and the information on these pages to fill it in. The first entry, on the Eskimos, has been done for you. Now do the others.

2 (a) Why do you think the Plains Indians rarely lived in groups of more than 500?
(b) Why were tipis that folded so useful?
(c) How do you think the arrival of the white settlers, railroad companies and guns destroyed their way of life?

3 (a) The Indians shared their land amongst the tribe. It was not owned by individuals. How do you think they felt about the white settlers' desire to own land?
(b) Why do you think living in desert regions had some advantages for the Indians of the south-west?

4 The movement of the south-eastern Indians to the west after 1830 was known as the 'Trail of Tears'. How did it get its name?

5 The Eskimo peoples had less contact with the white settlers than Indians elsewhere. What were the reasons for this?

The First Europeans

'In fourteen hundred and ninety-two Columbus sailed the ocean blue.'

Was Columbus the first European to discover America? Some people believe that the Viking Leif Ericsson reached Nova Scotia, on Canada's east coast, almost 500 years earlier, naming it Vinland. Other European nations have also claimed the discovery. But it was the voyages of Columbus, made on behalf of Spain, that made Europeans aware of the existence of the **New World**.

The Spaniards soon spread their empire of 'New Spain' across the area that is now California, Arizona, New Mexico, Texas and Florida. However, the east coast attracted most settlers, with the English, French, Dutch and Swedes competing fiercely for the land.

Most of this early settlement was concerned with trade. The French developed the fur trade in Canada, while the English grew tobacco in their **colony** of Virginia. Some settlements, however, were built by people escaping religious **persecution** in Europe. Among them were the 'Pilgrim Fathers' and their families, who landed near Cape Cod in 1620 from the ship 'Mayflower'. They were Puritans, a religious group then being persecuted in England. Their settlement of Massachusetts became the first self-governing colony in the land they called 'New England'.

Other religious groups settled the 'Middle Colonies' between Virginia and New England. William Penn, a member of a religious group called the Quakers, established the colony of Pennsylvania on land given to him by King Charles II. Catholics settled in nearby Maryland.

By 1733 there were 13 English colonies along the Atlantic coast. Each had its own government, money, trade laws and religious ways. The English language formed a link between them, but not everyone spoke it. Many other European settlers were also now arriving in search of freedom, especially the right to worship as they wished.

Today, most of these different nationalities have blended within the American way of life, but not all. Among the groups who have kept their original language and traditional way of life are the German people of Pennsylvania. Because their rules of dress do not permit ornaments, embroidery or collars, they wear plain, dark clothes that have earned them the name 'Plain People'. One of their groups, called the Amish, have the strictest rules to obey. They live very simply and work hard from dawn to dusk without the help of modern tools or equipment. Indoor plumbing, electricity, cars, radios, televisions and tractors are all banned. Their community spirit is especially strong. For example, if an Amish barn burns down, everyone helps to rebuild it the next day.

1 An Amish farmer of Pennsylvania using a team of horses to pull his plough. The Amish prefer not to use tractors or any other modern machines or gadgets to help them in their daily tasks.

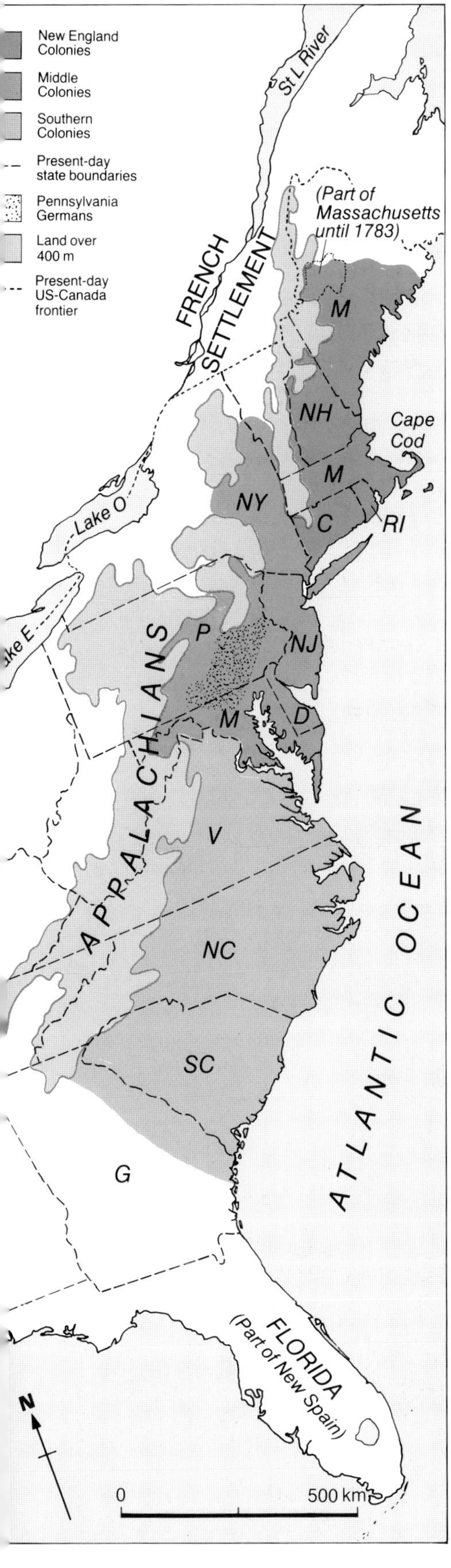
New England Colonies
Middle Colonies
Southern Colonies
Present-day state boundaries
Pennsylvania Germans
Land over 400 m
Present-day US-Canada frontier
St L River
FRENCH SETTLEMENT
(Part of Massachusetts until 1783)
M
NH
Cape Cod
M
NY
C
RI
Lake O
Lake E
P
NJ
M
D
APPALACHIANS
V
NC
SC
G
ATLANTIC OCEAN
FLORIDA (Part of New Spain)
N
0
500 km

2 (left) These are the 13 English colonies established along the Atlantic coast of North America by 1733. The present-day state boundaries are also shown.

3 (above) Jamestown was the first English settlement in North America. It started in 1607 from the simple stockade (wall of stakes) shown here.

1 The first Vikings to see North America were probably blown off course on their way to or from Greenland or Iceland. Evidence suggests that any Viking settlement there lasted only a short time. What do you think may have happened to the settlers?

2 Make a copy of picture 2. With the help of your atlas, name in full and mark on the 13 original English colonies. (Maine was part of the colony of Massachusetts.)

3 Working together in small groups, imagine you are a family leaving England in 1700 to start a new life in America.
(a) What will you take with you? (Remember space is limited on board ship.)
(b) Make a list of the things you will need to do as soon as you arrive.
(c) Plan out your first year's activities.
(d) What will your long-term plans include for the next five years?
(e) What do you think will be the main problems in carrying out your plans?

4 Imagine what it would be like to be part of an Amish family. Describe how your lifestyle would be different from what you are used to.

5 **Project idea:** It took the 'Mayflower' 65 days to cross the Atlantic. With unfavourable winds it took many other early travellers even longer. Today's luxury liners take only four or five days. In July 1952, the liner 'United States' did the voyage in only 3 days, 10 hours and 40 minutes to win the 'Blue Riband' for the fastest crossing. Try to explain why the crossing time varies so much. Find out more about everyday life on board a 17th-century ship, such as the 'Mayflower'.

The French Connection

The French arrived in North America about 12 years after Columbus. Breton fishermen began to catch cod off Nova Scotia and gradually moved up the St Lawrence River, where they traded for furs with local Indians. Trading posts grew along the river, and French explorers, such as Samuel de Champlain, mapped the surrounding area. In 1608 Champlain established Quebec, Canada's oldest city.

After the defeat of the Iroquois Indians in 1665, French exploration speeded up. La Salle explored the Great Lakes and, in 1682, sailed right down the Mississippi River to the Gulf of Mexico. He claimed the whole of the Mississippi Valley for King Louis XIV of France and named it 'Louisiana'.

The French built New Orleans, at the mouth of the Mississippi, 35 years later. Today, the city still shows its **multi-cultural** background, created not only by the French but also by Spanish, German, Irish and black **immigrants**. Other towns and cities in the area also recall their early links with the French. French-speaking Cajun people still live in Baton Rouge, Lafayette and other places. They are descendants of refugees who left Nova Scotia when France was forced to hand it over to Britain in 1713.

France lost the rest of its Canadian possessions to Britain in 1763. Although more than 200 years have gone by since then, French Canadians still have a great influence on the affairs of their country. Montreal, Canada's second largest city, has more French-speaking people than any other city in the world, except Paris. The province of Quebec is full of French place names. Over 80% of its population is of French origin. When Quebec became part of Canada in 1867, the people were allowed to keep their traditional way of life, including the French language.

Some 120 years later, the French Canadians of Quebec still feel strongly about their French connections. Some even want to make Quebec a separate country from the rest of Canada. As a result of this pressure, both French and English have been made official languages of Canada. Also, wherever there are enough French speakers, the people have the right to French schooling. There are French TV channels, and nearly all packaging is labelled in both languages.

1 The areas of eastern North America claimed by European nations in 1754. Ten years later, after defeat in war, France lost all its possessions to Britain and Spain.

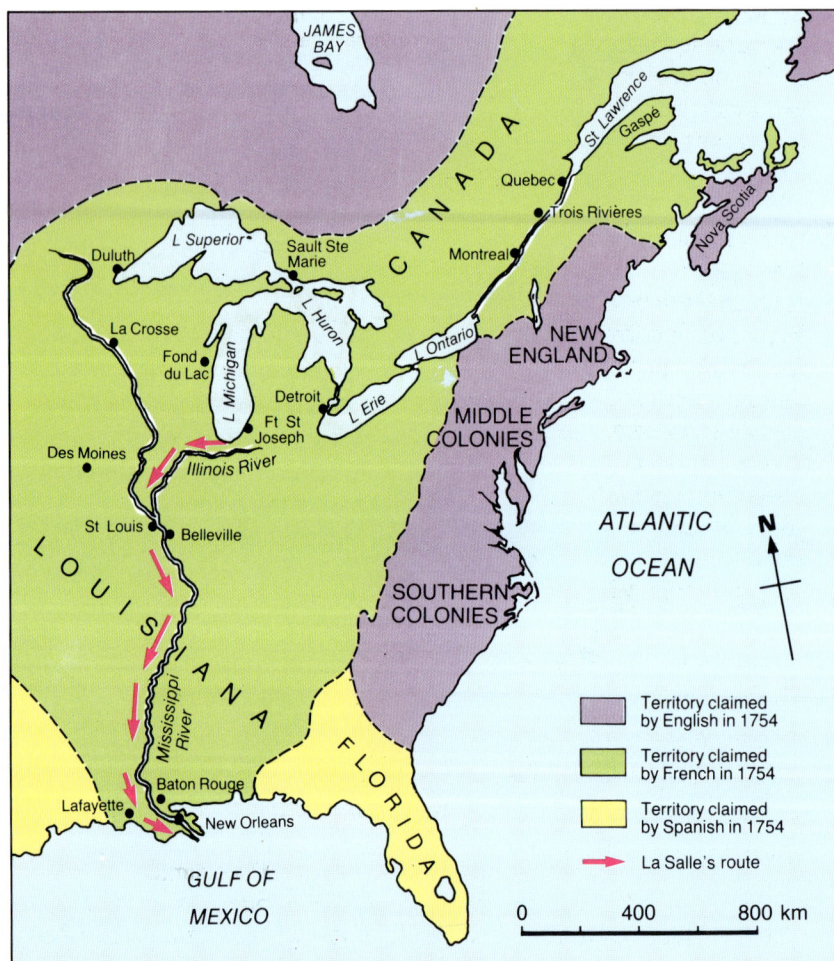

1 The areas of eastern North America claimed by European nations in 1754. Ten years later, after defeat in war, France lost all its possessions to Britain and Spain.

Territory claimed by English in 1754
Territory claimed by French in 1754
Territory claimed by Spanish in 1754
La Salle's route

0   400   800 km

1 Use picture 1 to help you to answer the following questions:
(a) When La Salle left Fort St Joseph in December 1681 there was snow on the ground and the Illinois River was frozen. How do you think he travelled and carried his supplies?
(b) By February, when he reached the Mississippi, the snow and ice were melting. How do you think this affected his method of transport?
(c) Work out the distance from Fort St Joseph to St Louis. If this part of the journey took about two months, roughly how far did he travel each day?
(d) Now work out the distance from St Louis to the Gulf of Mexico, which he reached in April 1682. How far did he travel on this part of the journey?
(e) Which method of transport was fastest, and why?
(f) Do you think his journey back to Canada would have been quicker or taken longer? Explain why.

2 Use your atlas to draw a map of Canada.
(a) Name the provinces and territories and their capital cities.
(b) Colour the province of Quebec in green.
(c) What would be the effect on Canada if Quebec became a separate country?
(d) How has the Canadian government tried to keep French speakers happy?

3 (a) Draw a pie chart using the figures below.

Anglo-Canadians (main language English)	61% (220°)
Franco-Canadians (main language French)	26% (94°)
Others (Dutch, Italian, German, Inuit, etc.)	13% (46°)

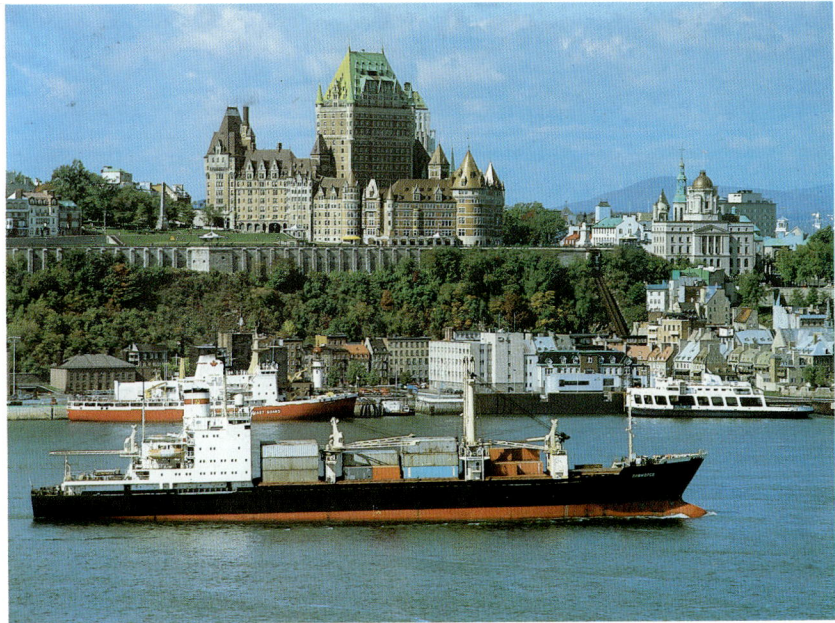

2 (above) The city of Quebec was established by the French nearly 380 years ago. The original settlement was sited high on the cliffs overlooking the St Lawrence River. This river is now a major seaway for international shipping.

3 (below) French and English are Canada's two official languages. Signs written in both languages are especially common in the province of Quebec. The largest number of French-speaking Canadians live in this part of Canada.

(b) Do you think having more than one main language in a country is helpful or makes problems. Explain and try to give examples.

4 The Spanish claimed much of North America, as picture 1 shows. Place names can often give an idea of who were the first people to settle there.
(a) Use your atlas to find place names in North America starting with Los, Las, El, San, Santa, or any other Spanish-sounding names. Mark them on your copy of a map of the USA.
(b) What does your map suggest about the main area of Spanish territory in North America?

Going West

purchase of Louisiana from France in 1803. This stretched from the Mississippi westward to the Rocky Mountains.

At first, only explorers and fur trappers ventured into this vast region and up into the Rockies. In 1812 they found the South Pass, the easiest route through the mountains to the west. By 1834 trappers had found their way to the Pacific coast and opened up the California Trail.

During the 1840s and 1850s, many thousands of pioneer families followed the hazardous trails across the mountains to begin new lives in the far west. In 1848 gold was discovered in California. The great Gold Rush was on. The next year tens of thousands of hopefuls known as 'Forty-niners' made their way to the west in search of their fortunes.

For some years, stagecoaches, riders of the Pony Express mail service and telegraph lines all

Today, it takes only about five hours to travel by air from New York to San Francisco. The journey has not always been so fast or as comfortable. Before the 1760s, few east-coast settlers travelled further west than the Appalachian Mountains. Then, Daniel Boone found a suitable route through the mountains at the Cumberland Gap.

In 1775, with 30 woodsmen, Boone began to clear the 'Wilderness Road', which ran

1 A pioneer family resting by their wagons during the long trek to the west in the 1850s.

some 500 km to Louisville. In just 15 years over 100 000 **pioneer** settlers left the crowded east coast for the new lands as far as the Mississippi River in the west.

Meanwhile, the 13 English colonies won their freedom from British rule in the War for Independence (1775–81) and became the United States of America. The new nation gained more land in the west with the

2 Routes to California and the west in the 1800s.

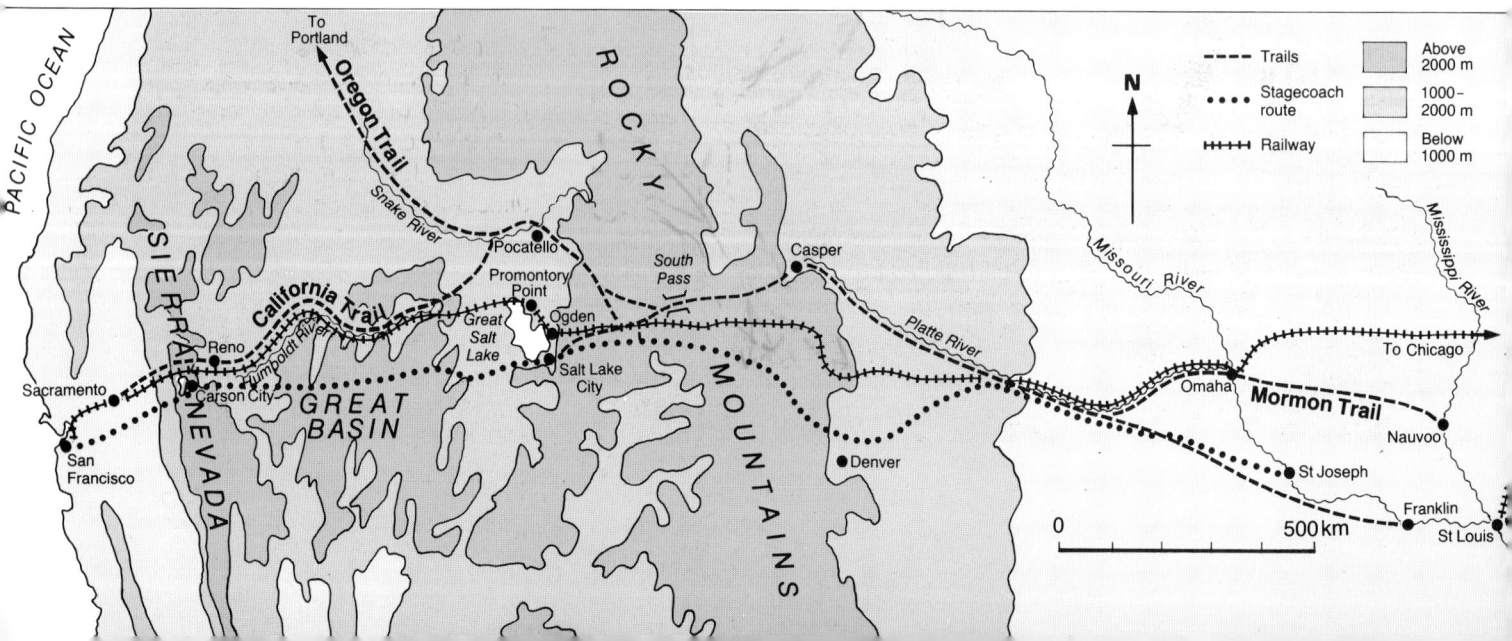

Legend:
- ---- Trails
- •••• Stagecoach route
- ++++ Railway
- Above 2000 m
- 1000–2000 m
- Below 1000 m

Westward by Wagon Train

Over 50 000 'Forty-niners' started their 3000 km trek to the west at the town of St Joseph. For the journey, most chose a covered wagon pulled by oxen or mules. They loaded up with a shotgun, pistol, nails, axe, pots and pans, water barrels, jug, lantern, candles, soap and a pick and pan. Flour, bacon, sugar, salt and coffee provided their basic diet. Various personal possessions completed the load.

With the winter snow melted and the new grass sprouting, they set off, often in teams of seven or eight wagons. The first 800 km of grassland and trees were easy going, although river crossings were difficult and sometimes dangerous. Covering 25 km a day, they soon reached the Rockies and South Pass. Ferocious storms and boggy ground forced them to dump precious possessions to lighten the wagons.

Next came the scorching desert of Utah and then, thankfully, the Humboldt River. For 500 km the trail clung to the river. Then, quite suddenly, the water turned a milky green and dried up in a revolting marsh. After drinking the water, many oxen died and people became ill with **dysentery**. With mid-summer temperatures up to 40 °C in the shade, some people went mad. Ahead lay 100 km of the waterless Humboldt Desert. Already at their limit, many people and animals did not make it, leaving a trail of abandoned equipment and skeletons.

The Tuckee and Carson Rivers offered fresh hope for those who survived. But the mountains of the Sierra Nevada lay ahead. Anyone who reached this point by early September stood a good chance of crossing into California before blizzards blocked the high passes.

Few 'Forty-niners' made their fortunes. The best claims had been staked long before they arrived.

followed similar routes to the west. Then, in 1869, a single event changed the future of the west – the first railway to cross the continent from the Atlantic to the Pacific was completed. Chinese crews working from the west and Irish gangers working from the east met at Promontory Point. They had laid 2800 km of track in only three years.

The 'Wild West' often seen in cowboy films lasted only from about the 1860s to the 1890s. It was a lawless time when the gun ruled. It has left a long list of heroes and villains, such as Wyatt Earp, Jesse James, Billy the Kid, 'Wild Bill' Hickok and many more, most of whom met with a violent end.

3 The ceremony marking the completion of the first railway to cross the USA from east to west. In 1869 the eastern and western sections of the railway were joined together at Promontory Point in the Utah desert. The line now takes a route further south across the Great Salt Lake.

1 Why do you think that most early settlers stayed fairly close to the east coast? How did the 'Wilderness Road' help to change this?

2 Read through the equipment and supplies given in the box on the left.
(a) Briefly explain why each piece of equipment was important on such a journey.
(b) The supplies do not include food for the animals. How do you think they survived?
(c) What would you have taken along on the journey as personal possessions?

3 (a) Suggest reasons for travelling in small groups of wagons rather than alone or in a bigger wagon train.
(b) If the wagon teams averaged about 20 km a day during their journey, how long would it take them to reach California from St Joseph?
(c) Suggest how the physical environment, such as rivers, mountains, deserts, vegetation and climate, both helped and hindered the wagon trains on the journey.

4 Why do you think the Chinese worked on the western section of the railway and the Irish on the eastern part? [Hint: Look at a map of the world.]

5 Despite the difficulties, the railway was built very quickly.
(a) Work out the average length of track laid each day.
(b) Describe some of the difficulties that faced the railway builders.

6 **Project idea:** Choose one famous personality from the 'Wild West' and find out as much as you can about his or her life and times.

Slavery and Civil War

1 Rich plantation owners in the southern states often lived in fine mansions. 'Oak Alley', built in the 1830s, stands by the Mississippi River just above New Orleans. In those days, steamboats carried sugar from the plantations upriver to the industrial northern states, and cotton downriver for export overseas.

2 The 'Underground Railroad' was a system of escape routes used by black slaves fleeing from the southern states before the American Civil War.

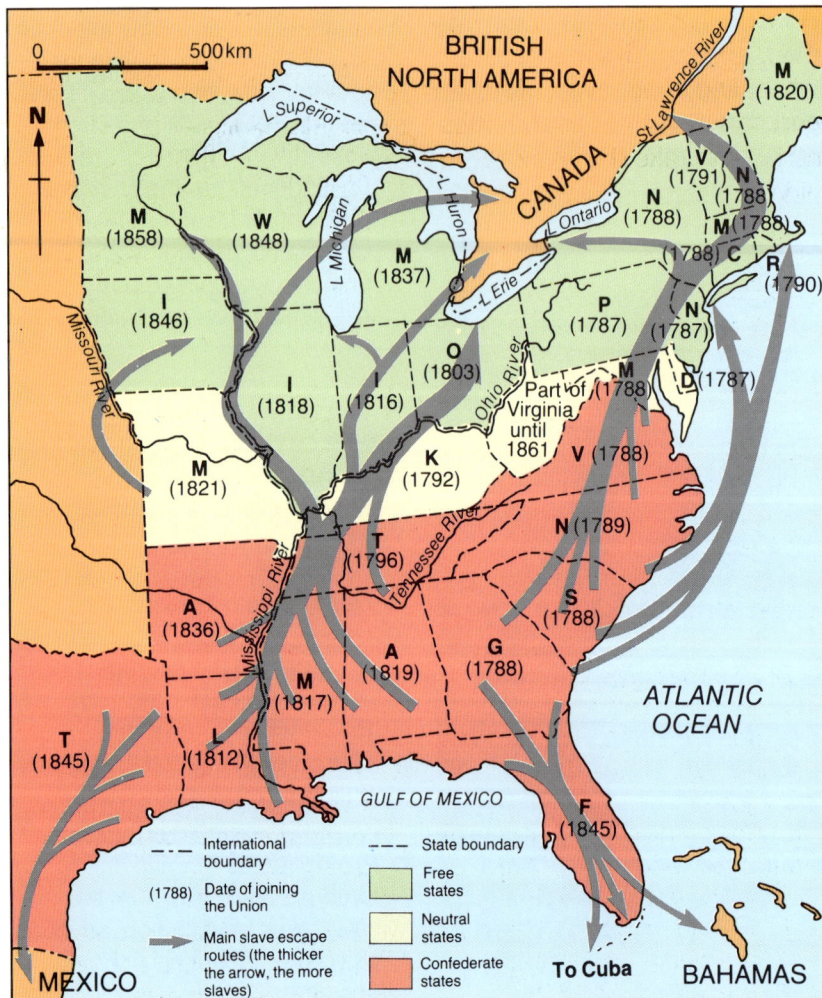

'We hold ... that all Men are created equal, that they are endowed by their Creator with certain unalienable Rights, that among these are Life, Liberty, and the Pursuit of Happiness.'

With these words, the 13 east coast colonies made their Declaration of Independence from British rule on 4 July 1776. But in the new United States of America all men were certainly not equal and free. **Plantation** owners in the southern states used black slave labour to grow rice, tobacco, indigo, cotton and sugar. The slaves were brought across the Atlantic Ocean from Africa in cramped and overcrowded ships for sale in the Americas. This trade was made illegal in 1808. There were already enough black slaves in North America. They made up over half the population of Virginia and North and South Carolina.

3 The movement of black people within the USA between 1870 and 1980. The numbers represent thousands. A minus (−) sign means people leaving. A plus (+) sign means people arriving.

Years	South	North	West
1870–80	−60	+60	−
1880–90	−70	+70	−
1890–1900	−170	+170	−
1900–10	−170	+150	+20
1910–20	−450	+420	+30
1920–30	−750	+710	+40
1930–40	−350	+300	+50
1940–50	−1600	+1080	+340
1950–60	−1470	+1040	+290
1960–70	−1380	+990	+300
1970–80	+210	−340	+130

Many people in the northern states did not like slavery. Tens of thousands of slaves escaped from the south to freedom in the north. From 1830 to 1860 they were helped by an operation known as the 'Underground Railroad' (see picture 2). Disagreement between the northern and southern states became stronger. In 1861, 11 southern states broke away from the United States, or 'Union', to form their own 'Confederacy'. President Abraham Lincoln said this was illegal and sent Union troops into the south. He expected a quick victory.

The **Civil War** that followed dragged on for four years. Before the north finally won, thousands had died. The south – known as the 'Cotton Kingdom' – was destroyed and the plantation system finished. Four million black slaves were freed but they were still not equal. President Lincoln's words at the end of the war showed what many white Americans felt about black people: 'Neither my own feelings nor those of the mass of whites will admit of making them social and political equals.'

Since the 1880s blacks have officially had equal rights according to US law. But in practice few of them have had the same opportunities as most whites to get adequate schooling, medical care, housing, or well-paid jobs. Until 1954 black and white children even had to attend separate schools. Even today, few black children can expect the same opportunities as most white children.

4 The group of people called the Ku Klux Klan often holds demonstrations against black people and other minority groups in the southern states. Its members may even use violence to support their belief in the superiority of white people. They use the old flag of the Confederacy to show their liking for the traditional southern way of life.

Not only blacks but also **minority groups**, such as **Hispanics** and Asians, suffer **racial discrimination**. In America, as in Britain, they often live in the poorest parts of towns and cities and have to take the less well-paid jobs.

In 1978 the average white family earned $18 368 a year, the average black family $10 879. Almost 25% of unemployed people in 1980 were black, although blacks make up only about 12% of the American population. Also, a higher proportion of black children suffer from malnutrition than white children.

1 Look at picture 2.
(a) Describe the directions in which the slaves escaped.
(b) To which countries did they escape?
(c) The 'Neutral States' were actually slave states. Suggest why they did not join the Confederacy in the Civil War.
(d) What problems faced the black slaves when they were freed at the end of the Civil War?

2 On your own copy of a map showing the states of the USA:
(a) Name all the states shown in picture 2, plus California and Oregon.
(b) Colour the states that joined the Union before 1800 in red; between 1800 and 1830 in yellow; and between 1830 and 1860 in blue (also California, 1850, and Oregon, 1859).

(c) Your map shows the growth of the USA up to 1860. Describe how it grew.

3 (a) Use the figures in picture 3 to draw three line graphs showing the movements of black people within the USA between 1870 and 1980. Pick different colours for north, south and west and use the same axes so that you can easily compare your results.
(b) Describe the patterns shown on your graph and suggest reasons for them.

4 Use the information in the box to write about the sort of problems you think still face black people in the USA.

5 **Project idea:** You are a slave on a plantation. Write a story about your life and your escape.

The Melting Pot

1 Many North American cities have districts in which particular ethnic groups live. This is the Chinatown district of San Francisco. It contains many colourful oriental shops, restaurants and signs. New York and Vancouver also have large Chinese communities.

By the 1890s some people were saying that the USA had become a huge 'melting pot' in which immigrants from nations all over the world were being mixed together. It was hoped that Europeans, Asians, Africans, and Central and South Americans would all become simply 'Americans'. So they have, but they have also kept many of the traditional ways of life of their original countries.

Many Irish Americans march each year in St Patrick's Day parades, Chinese Americans celebrate the Chinese New Year and German Americans hold Oktoberfests. Folklife festivals encourage the traditional crafts, foods, music, dances and costumes from the homelands of many of these **ethnic groups**. For example, some 6000 Texans from 30 such groups take part in the Texas Folklife Festival, held in San Antonio every August. Among them are Greeks, Lebanese, Scots, Mexicans, Poles, Balinese, Irish and American Indians. Most of these people have broad Texas accents and were born in the USA.

Whatever their origins, not all Americans have the same standard of living or opportunities. Most of the first immigrants, as picture 3 shows, were Europeans. Many of them arrived in New York and settled in the larger towns and cities, where they could find work. They became an important supply of cheap labour for America's growing industries.

A lot of the new arrivals, especially those from southern and eastern Europe, found low-rent housing near the city centres and grouped together with others who spoke their language. These crowded, run-down areas were called **ghettos**.

During and after the First World War, thousands of southern blacks arrived in the northern cities. As the city centres were already crowded, they found low-rent homes further out. South Side in Chicago, Harlem in New York and Roxbury in Boston became black ghettos.

In recent years, it has been Asians and, particularly, Hispanics who have moved into low-rent areas and low-paid jobs in the cities. In 1980 there were officially almost 15 million Hispanics in the USA, 80% of them from Mexico. California, Texas, Illinois, New York and Massachusetts now include the Spanish language in their educational programmes. Miami, in Florida, accepts both English and Spanish as official languages.

People cannot just go and live in the USA. They have to get permission from the US government. There are now strict controls on immigration. On the border with Mexico, for example, there are regular patrols. Every year they catch hundreds of people trying to get into the USA without permits and return them to Mexico. Even so, it is thought that up to six million people have entered the country by illegal routes.

2 The origins of immigrants entering Canada in 1965 and 1980. The proportions are given in degrees of a circle to help you draw the pie chart in question 3.

Country of origin	1965	1980
Europe		
UK and Ireland	97	50
Italy	65	4
Germany	18	11
Portugal	14	14
Other European	65	18
The Americas		
USA	40	25
West Indies	7	22
Asia	29	169
Others	25	47
Total	360	360

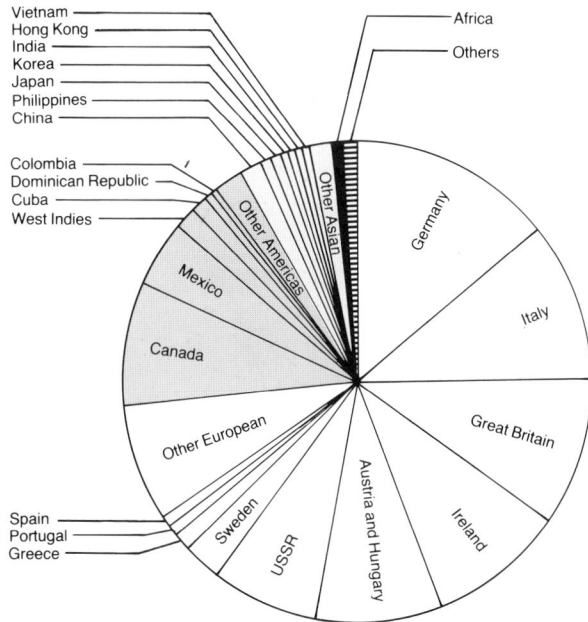

3 The origins of immigrants entering the USA between 1820 and 1979.

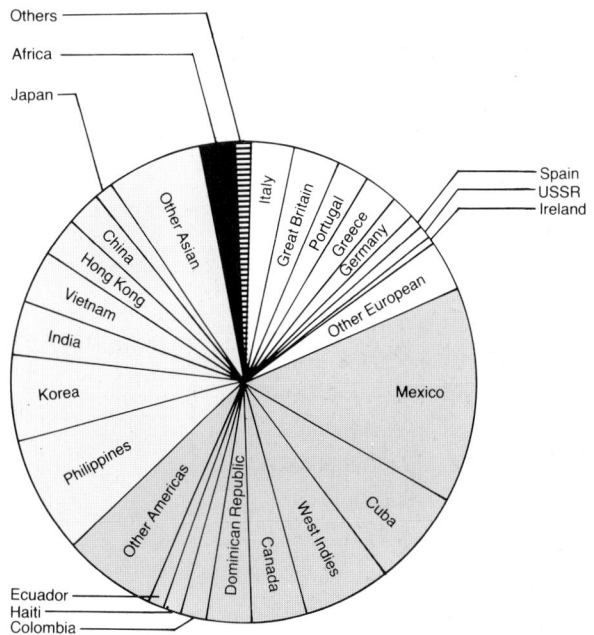

4 The origins of immigrants entering the USA between 1971 and 1979.

5 Over 1300 km of the frontier between the USA and Mexico is formed by the river known as the Rio Grande. Every year, large numbers of Mexicans cross it and enter the USA illegally. Many simply wade across the shallow water between the neighbouring cities of Juarez and El Paso.

1 Suggest some reasons why many immigrants group together.

2 Look at picture 3. This pie chart shows the origins of the 49 million people who arrived in the USA between 1820 and 1979.
(a) Write down the five countries that provided most immigrants.
(b) Write down the continent that provided most immigrants, and estimate roughly what proportion came from it.
(c) Try to explain why there are over 26 million blacks, most of them with African ancestry, in the USA, but so few in the chart. (Page 20 may help.)

Now look at picture 4. This pie chart shows the origin of the four million immigrants arriving in the 1970s.

(d) Write down the five countries that provided most immigrants.
(e) Write down the continent that provided most recent immigrants.
(f) Compare both charts and describe the changes that have

taken place recently in the pattern of immigration.
(g) Suggest reasons for these changes .

3 Use picture 2 to draw two pie charts showing immigration into Canada in 1965 and 1980. (The numbers are in degrees to help you.) Describe the changes in Canada's pattern of immigration.

4 (a) About 25% of Hispanics live below the official poverty level (the national average is about 12% of all people in the USA). What does this tell you about the standard of living of many Hispanics? Try to explain this situation.
(b) Why do you think that so many Mexicans risk trying to enter the USA illegally?

5 The US government now limits the number of immigrants. Write a few paragraphs explaining what you think about this, imagining you are (a) a US government official, (b) an illegal immigrant.

23

The Big Apple

Between 1900 and 1910 up to 15 000 immigrants a day landed in New York, America's 'Gateway City'. They were on their way to what they hoped would be a new and better life. In 1907 alone, a million people passed through the immigration centre on Ellis Island, in New York Harbour. Today, about seven million people live in New York City, with another nine million in the surrounding **urban area**.

New York is North America's greatest port. It has a naturally sheltered, deep-water harbour, which is easily reached from the open sea. In 1980 it handled goods worth $44 000 million. This was almost twice the amount handled by Houston, in second place. New York is also the 'business capital' of the USA. About 75 of the 500 largest **industrial corporations** have their headquarters in New York City. In the 1950s there were even more.

Most people will have their own idea of what New York is like. They will think of the Empire State Building, Central Park, Broadway, the Statue of Liberty, Wall Street, Times Square, the United Nations Building and many more famous sights. All of these are in Manhattan, which is only one of the five boroughs that make up New York City. The others are the Bronx, Brooklyn, Queens and Staten Island.

New York is a city of great contrasts and is always changing. The skyscrapers of

1 The towering office buildings of Lower Manhattan make New York the business capital of America. The twin towers of the World Trade Center (top left) reach 420 m into the sky and provide about 840 000 m^2 of office space. There are also more than 50 shops, 20 restaurants and a hotel in the Center.

2 The ghettos of Harlem, north of Central Park, show how hard it is for many black people to escape from poverty and bad housing conditions.

Manhattan represent its great wealth, while not far away can be found the black ghettos of Harlem. When a new ten-lane highway was built through Sunset Park, Brooklyn, middle-income families of Polish and Scandinavian origin moved out. Low-income Puerto Ricans moved into the houses they left. Across the Hudson River, in Jersey City, it is the Puerto Ricans who are moving out as old houses are improved and their prices go up.

This process of renovation is gradually changing the character of some old areas. For example, in SoHo, Manhattan, old buildings are being turned into smart antique shops, restaurants and artists' studios.

All over New York City many ethnic groups still tend to live in separate areas. Roman Catholic priests in Brooklyn celebrate mass in 14 different languages!

3 The main ethnic communities in Brooklyn. The percentage figures show the proportion of the borough's total population made up by each group.

4 The crowded beach at Coney Island in the New York borough of Brooklyn. Brooklyn once had more seaside resorts than any other American city. Today, most of the amusement parks, theatres and fine hotels have gone. But on a hot day, half a million New Yorkers may go to this beach.

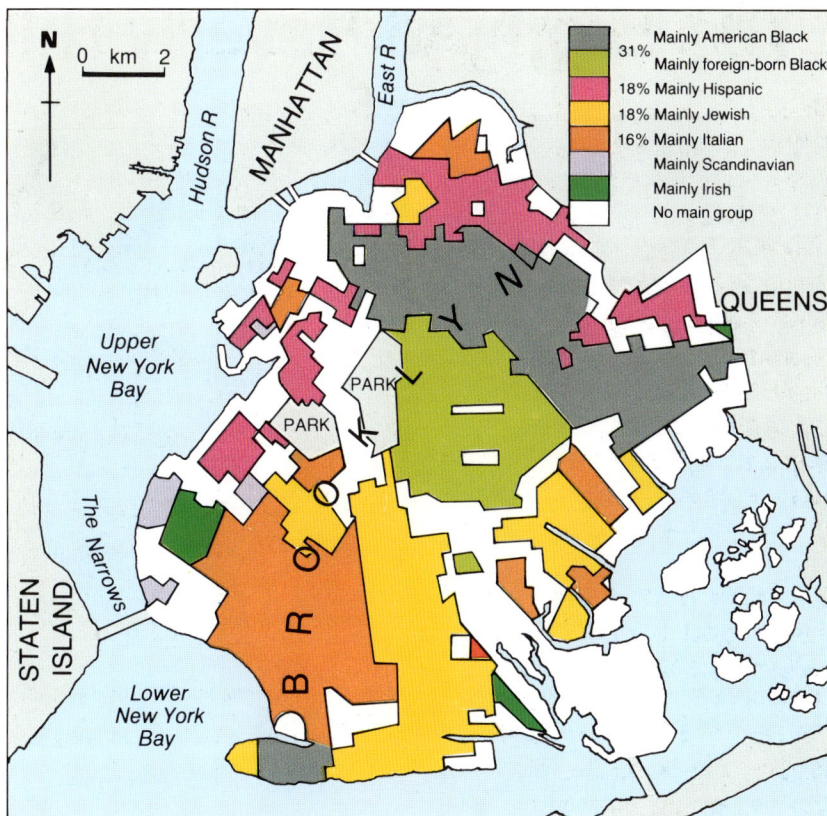

1 From 1892 to 1954 Ellis Island was the reception centre for all newly arrived immigrants. Here their names were recorded and they were given medical checks. About eight out of ten were then let into the USA, the rest sent home. Why was Ellis Island called 'The Island of Tears'.

2 Manhattan is an island of solid rock. Today, land prices in the downtown area are high, and space is limited. How do these facts explain the skyline shown in picture 1?

3 New York is also known for its muggings, vandalism, drugs, vice, racial problems and traffic jams. Use the pictures here, your impressions from films or TV and any other information you can find to describe the good and bad things about New York City.

4 The Brooklyn Dodgers baseball club moved to Los Angeles in 1957. Since 1960 some industrial corporations have moved their headquarters away from New York. In the 1970s almost 450 000 jobs were lost, and since 1970 about a million people have left the city. Give reasons for these changes.

5 Many residential areas of New York change in character as higher and lower-income families move in and out. Try to explain why this happens.

6 **Project idea:** Working in small groups, choose different topics about New York City. Collect as much information as you can on the topic you have chosen, including pictures, drawings and written material, and make a wall display.

The Bronx to Beverly Hills

1 In the Bronx, as in many other city ghettos, there is much poverty and substandard housing.

2 A luxury home in Hollywood, complete with an expensive car, is a dream that only the rich can make come true. Many famous film stars have lived in houses like this one in nearby Beverly Hills.

The invention of the motor car and the development of public transport systems in the early 1900s made a great difference to the way people lived in American cities. People began to move out of the old, run-down city centres to live in newer districts further out. These districts, or suburbs, are more pleasant and less crowded, but living there costs more. So better-off white families generally live there, while the lower-income black families and other minority groups remain in the inner city.

For some, the dream of great wealth comes true. The very rich live in big, air-conditioned mansions in such places as Beverly Hills, a suburb of Los Angeles. Here they can relax by their swimming pools or play tennis on their own private courts. Many famous film stars from the nearby Hollywood studios have had luxurious homes in this area.

In contrast, many other people live in old, poorly maintained and substandard housing in city ghettos, such as those in the Bronx in New York City. Poor housing and poverty also exist in many **rural areas**, where there are fewer job opportunities. Such areas include many of the Indian reservations.

About 75% of all North Americans live in towns and cities. In the USA, this urban area takes up only about 15% of the land, in Canada even less. Europeans notice that towns and cities in North America have their own special character that makes them different from those in Europe. Yet they are also very different from each other. One very American feature is that the buildings are less crowded together than in Britain and most of Europe. North American towns and cities therefore tend to spread over much larger areas. So people have to make longer journeys to work or to the town centre. One result of this has been the development of very large supermarkets, shopping 'plazas' and 'malls' in the suburbs.

3 Megalopolis: this almost continuous urban and suburban area stretches for nearly 800 km along America's Atlantic coast. More than 40 million people live there.

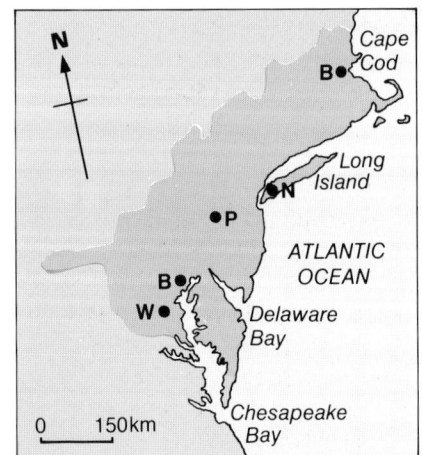

4 This type of huge shopping centre, with its enormous car-park, became popular in North America long before the first one was built in Britain.

5 Although there is no such thing as a typical American town, this small-town street scene shows many of the things that make most of them different from towns in Britain.

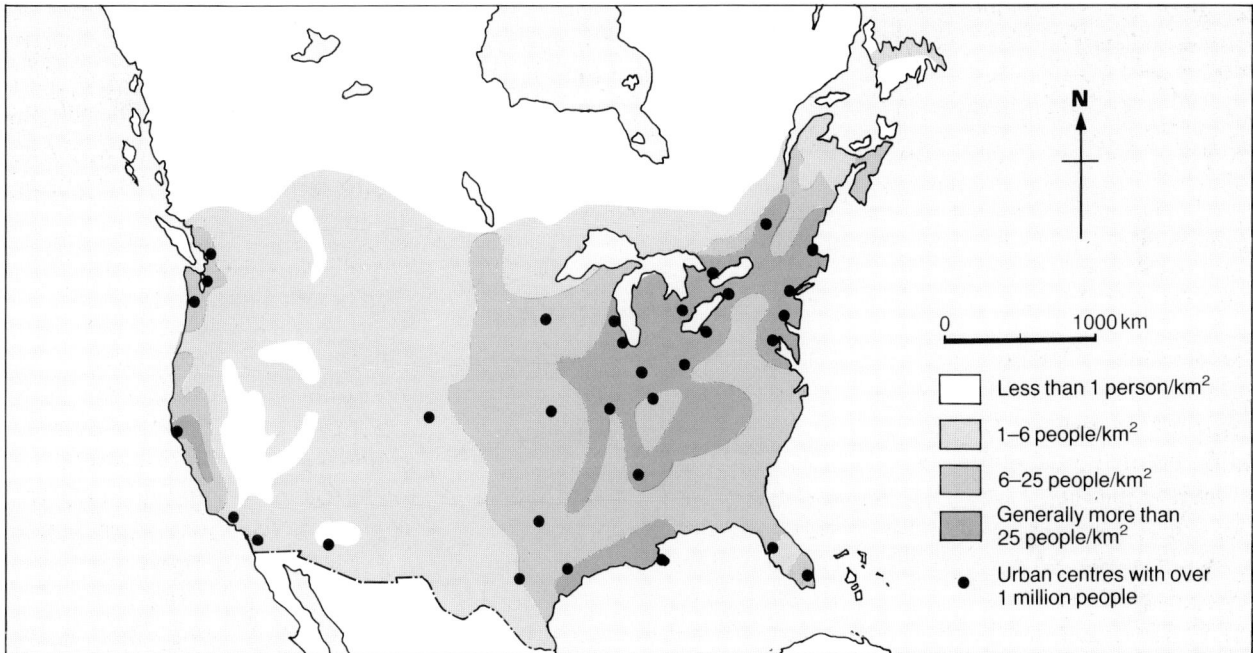

N

0   1000 km

☐ Less than 1 person/km²

☐ 1–6 people/km²

☐ 6–25 people/km²

☐ Generally more than 25 people/km²

● Urban centres with over 1 million people

1 Look at picture 5. Write down all the things that make this American town different from a town you know in Britain.

2 Where would you rather live, in the inner city area or the suburbs? Give reasons for your choice.

3 Picture 4 shows a large suburban supermarket and shopping mall. List the advantages and disadvantages of shopping here. Why do you think such shopping centres became popular in North America long before they were built in Britain?

4 In what ways do pictures 1 and 2 show the great contrasts that can be found in North America?

5 Make a copy of picture 3 and use an atlas to name the five main cities. If the population of the USA is about 220 million, roughly what proportion lives in this area?

6 Look at picture 6.
(a) Is the population evenly or unevenly spread?
(b) The way people are spread is called their 'distribution'. Briefly describe the pattern of distribution shown on the map.
(c) Using your atlas, try to

6 The distribution of population .

suggest reasons why some areas have less than one person per square kilometre. (Look at maps showing climate, relief and natural vegetation.)

7 Draw a divided bar chart to show the types of job people do in the USA. Use these figures:

Agriculture	4%
Industry	31%
Services	65%

How does this pattern of employment fit in with the fact that about 75% of North Americans live in urban areas?

Farming the Prairies

Bigger farms, more machines and higher **yields**. This is the way North American farming has changed in the last 100 years. Canada and the USA now produce enough food to feed themselves and to sell to other countries. They put a great deal of money into farming and into processing and selling food. Americans call this 'agribusiness'.

The North American prairies were once vast plains of grass.

Tall grasses grew in the eastern part, shorter and more wiry kinds in the western areas. Huge herds of buffalo roamed the grasslands and were hunted by the Plains Indians.

Early settlers from the east found farming on the prairies difficult. The thick turf, or sod, was hard to plough. Known as 'sodbusters', these hardy people were **subsistence farmers**, who grew only enough for themselves and their families. Survival was often a struggle.

Meanwhile, ranchers were moving in with cattle driven north along trails from Texas and Mexico. Sometimes the cowboys and farmers argued over their claims to the land. Fences were torn down and crops damaged. In the end, the ranchers settled on the western prairies, as better farm machinery allowed more and more land in the eastern prairies to be ploughed up for growing crops.

The prairies are a long way from the coastal ports. So it was not

1 The prairies of North America. The 'tall-grass' prairies in the east were difficult to cultivate until the introduction of the steel plough in 1837. Indian attacks and harsh winters in the north also made life difficult. Today, the tall grass has gone and the area has become one of the most productive agricultural regions in the world. One major problem has been **soil erosion**. This has been reduced by using a cultivator that cuts the roots of weeds about 5 cm below the ground, but does not break up and turn over the soil like a plough. As a result, the soil is less likely to become dry and loose and so blow away.

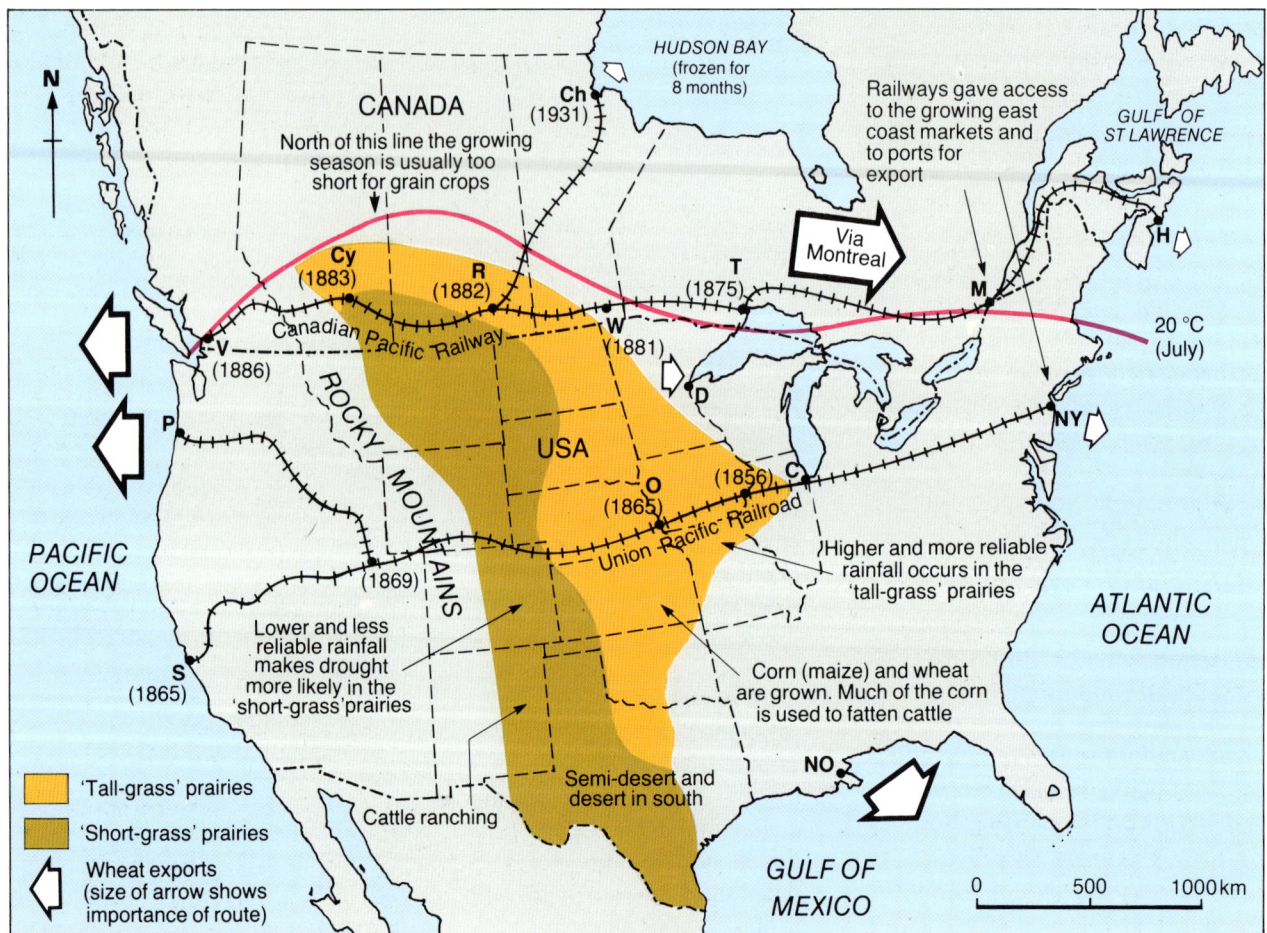

2 As far as the eye can see, the flat, open spaces of the prairies are divided into a regular patchwork of fields, as in this view around a farmhouse in Kansas.

until the railway network grew that farming became really important there. The US and Canadian governments and the railway companies attracted more farmers to the area by offering them 65 ha plots of land for only a few dollars. These original plots were square and gave the prairies their characteristic chessboard appearance. Farming became commercial, because the farmers now grew crops for sale rather than just for themselves.

Today, a lot of maize and sorghum is grown on the prairies for fattening pigs and cattle ready for market. Some of the cattle come from the ranches in the west. Wheat is an important crop in many states and across the border in Canada. It is sold to many parts of the world and also sent where there is famine.

Only 8% of Canada's land area is used for farming. Difficult **relief**, poor soils and unsuitable climate limit the area that can be farmed. About 75% of Canada's farmland is in the southern parts of the three 'Prairie Provinces'. These produce about 20 million tonnes of wheat a year.

1 The prairies were first used for hunting, then subsistence farming and finally commercial agriculture. Describe each of these uses in your own words.

2 Draw your own map showing the boundaries of the USA states and Canadian provinces. Using your atlas and picture 1:
(a) Colour in the tall-grass and short-grass prairies.
(b) Name all the states and provinces covered by the prairies.
(c) Draw on the railways and mark and name the cities shown.
(d) Colour the Rocky Mountains brown.
(e) Draw red arrows from ports that may export wheat to Asian countries, and blue arrows from those that may export it to Europe.

3 How do you think that inventions such as the steel plough, the freezing of meat, and barbed wire helped to change prairie farming?

4 Try to explain why the farmers needed the railways and the railways needed the farmers. How does this help to explain the low price of the 65 ha plots offered to farmers?

5 Use picture 3 and any other information to describe the effects of more and bigger machines on North American agriculture.

6 **Project idea:** Soil erosion has been a great problem on the prairies. Find out more about the damage it has done and the ways farmers are trying to prevent it.

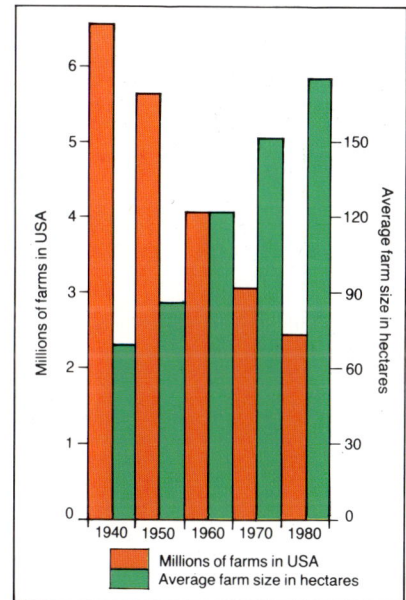

3 The changing pattern of US farms. Similar changes have taken place in Canada, where average farm sizes grew from 95 to 200 ha between 1940 and 1980.

Truck Farming

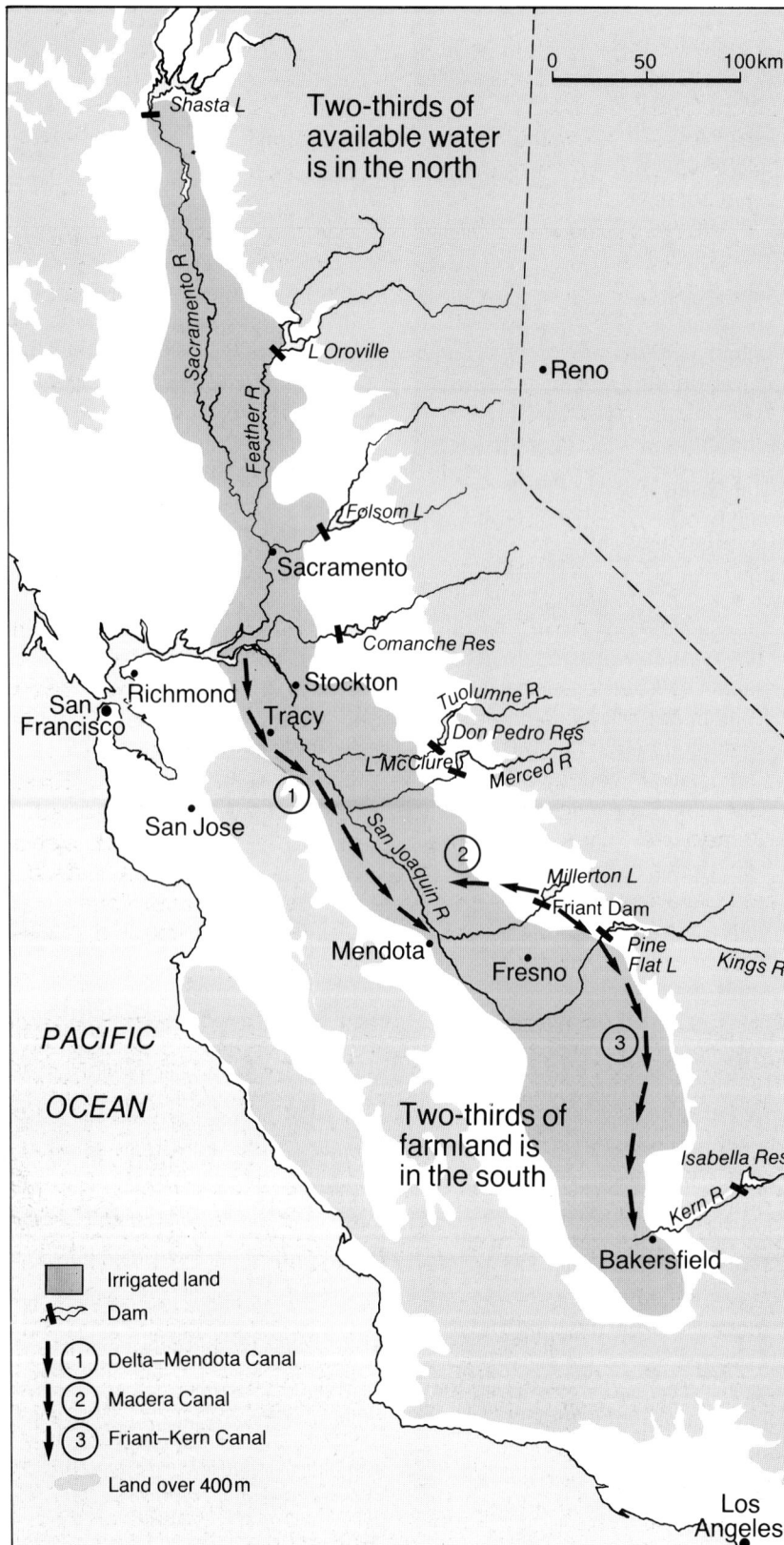

Two-thirds of available water is in the north

| 0 | 50 | 100km |

Shasta L

Sacramento R

L Oroville

• Reno

Feather R

Folsom L

Sacramento

Comanche Res

Richmond
Stockton
San Francisco
Tracy

Tuolumne R

Don Pedro Res

① L McClure

Merced R

San Joaquin R

②

San Jose

Millerton L
Friant Dam

Mendota•

Pine Flat L

Kings R

Fresno

PACIFIC

③

OCEAN

Two-thirds of farmland is in the south

Isabella Res

Kern R

Bakersfield

Irrigated land

Dam

① Delta–Mendota Canal

② Madera Canal

③ Friant–Kern Canal

Land over 400m

Los Angeles

Many people prefer fresh vegetables to canned or frozen ones. City dwellers generally cannot grow their own vegetables but have to buy them. Many vegetables go off quickly or are easily bruised. So they are often grown near to the towns and cities where they are to be eaten. That is why the east coast of the USA from Maryland to Long Island is an important vegetable-growing area. New York, Philadelphia and other large cities are nearby. Road and rail communications are good.

This type of farming is very specialized. It needs a lot of **inputs**, including money, labour, equipment and fertilizers. It also produces high crop yields from fairly small areas of land. So it is an **intensive** method of cultivation. In North America it is called 'truck farming'.

Truck farming is also found along the eastern shores of Lakes Michigan, Erie and Ontario, close to large, industrial cities. The 'Winter Garden' of Florida and the Gulf Coast produces fresh winter vegetables and early-season fruits, while snow is still on the ground further north. Smaller areas of truck farming are also found near other large urban centres.

By 1980 almost half the vegetables grown in the USA

1 The Central Valley Project is a vast irrigation scheme in California. It carries water from the wetter northern part of the state to the drier farmlands of the south.

came from California, most of them from the Central Valley. Until the early 1900s, this region was too dry for growing fruit or vegetables, and the land was used for wheat farms and cattle ranches. Then falling grain prices, better methods of **irrigation** and refrigerated rail transport changed the pattern of farming.

The most important irrigation scheme in California is the Central Valley Project. It was started in 1937 and took 14 years to complete. It prevents winter flooding in the Sacramento Valley and carries much-needed water to the San Joaquin Valley further south. Altogether, the project controls over 2 million ha of irrigated farmland.

Irrigation in the Central Valley has allowed farmers to use more intensive methods of farming. This needs **seasonal field labour**, which is provided mostly by Mexicans and Filipinos. The Californian truck farms have also needed to be well organized in order to compete with other areas producing vegetables. Strict quality control, hard bargaining for low transport costs, and much advertising are important parts of the Californian agribusiness. Taken by refrigerated transport, fresh produce from California is now sold thousands of kilometres from the farms where it is grown. You may see some in your local supermarket.

2 Immigrant workers harvesting tomatoes on a truck farm in California.

1 (a) How do you think truck farming may have got its name?
(b) What is it called in Britain?

2 (a) Why are good communications so important for truck farming?
(b) Why is so much labour used at harvest time rather than just machines?
(c) Why has refrigerated rail transport been particularly helpful to California?

3 On your own copy of a map of the Central Valley:
(a) Colour the canals in blue and the irrigated land in green.
(b) Shade the land over 400 m in brown and use an atlas to label the mountains of the Sierra Nevada and Coast Ranges.
(c) Add the following routes in red to represent main roads and railways:
(i) The Interstate Highway runs from Los Angeles along the western edge of the irrigated area to Tracy. It then goes to Sacramento and follows the same route as the railway along the western edge of the irrigated area up past Shasta Lake.
(ii) The highway and railway also leave Sacramento for Reno and then continue in a north-easterly direction.
(iii) Sacramento is also linked to Richmond by road and rail.
(iv) Another major road and the railway join Bakersfield, Fresno, Stockton, Tracy, Richmond, San Jose and San Francisco.

4 With the help of picture 1 and other information on these pages, copy out and complete the paragraph below.

Small dams along the ... side of the valley store water from the spring snow melt in the ... ... mountains. This stops ... and allows the water to be used during the summer. Unfortunately, two-thirds of the ... ... is in the north, while two-thirds of the ... is in the south. So water flowing south in the ... River is diverted to Tracy. Here it is raised 60 m into the ... ... It is carried 160 km south to ... , where it flows into the ... ... River. This replaces the water stored behind the ... Dam, which is sent along the ... ... to Bakersfield in the very dry south. Over ... ... of farmland is irrigated, thanks to the ... ...

31

Motor City

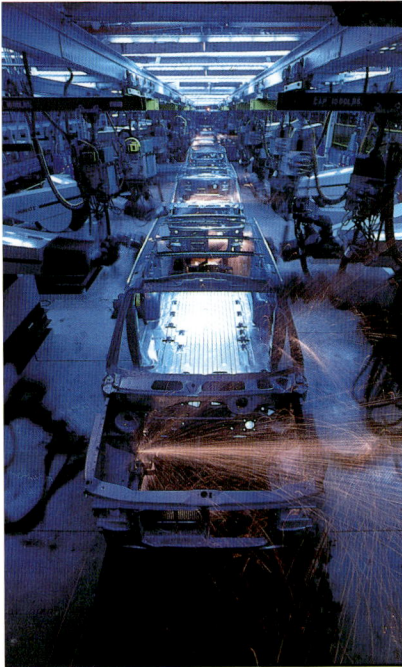

1 Robots assembling cars at a factory in Detroit. Modern methods of car-making use more machines and fewer people than in the past. One result of this has been rising unemployment in the car industry.

Millions of cars at a low price so that everybody could own one. That was Henry Ford's aim when he formed the Ford Motor Company in Detroit in 1903. He made cars that were exactly the same as each other by using **standardized parts**.

Each car was built bit by bit as it moved along the **assembly line**. Everyone had a place on the assembly line and a particular task. This meant that people with little training and only a few skills could do the job. The assembly line speeded up production and lowered costs. As cars got cheaper, more people could afford to buy them.

There were some 50 car manufacturers in these early years, but most were unable to compete with the bigger companies. General Motors of Detroit, founded in 1908, gradually took over such famous makes as Buick, Cadillac, Chevrolet, Oldsmobile and Pontiac. Today, General Motors, Ford and Chrysler together build over 95% of cars made in the United States.

By 1910, most of America's fast-growing car industry had been attracted to Detroit. Steel was available from neighbouring towns and cities on the Great Lakes, and the major markets of the east coast could be reached via the Erie Canal. Skilled workers from the earlier carriage and wagon builders were also available. But these reasons alone do not fully explain why Detroit became 'Motor City'. Chance also played a part. Henry Ford was born nearby, and William Durant chose the city as the headquarters of what was to be the largest car-making company in the world: General Motors.

The car is very much a part of everyday life in North America. 'Drive-ins' allow people to stay in their cars while they eat, visit the bank, watch 'movies' and even worship.

Living in a big country, Americans always preferred big, comfortable, powerful cars and cheap 'gasoline' (petrol). But this has changed. In the 1970s the cost of petrol rose sharply. Arab oil producers had raised their prices, and Iran, once an important source of oil for the USA, had plunged into a revolution. Americans suddenly wanted smaller cars that used less 'gas'. American manufacturers were not ready to meet the demand. Their car sales fell as more and more small Japanese cars were imported. In 1980, after 76 years as the world's number one producer, the USA was overtaken by Japan.

2 The proportion of American and foreign cars sold in the USA in 1970 and 1982. Because of an overall drop in car sales and an increase in imported cars, American car-makers had to shut factories and to modernize their methods. Both have resulted in fewer jobs.

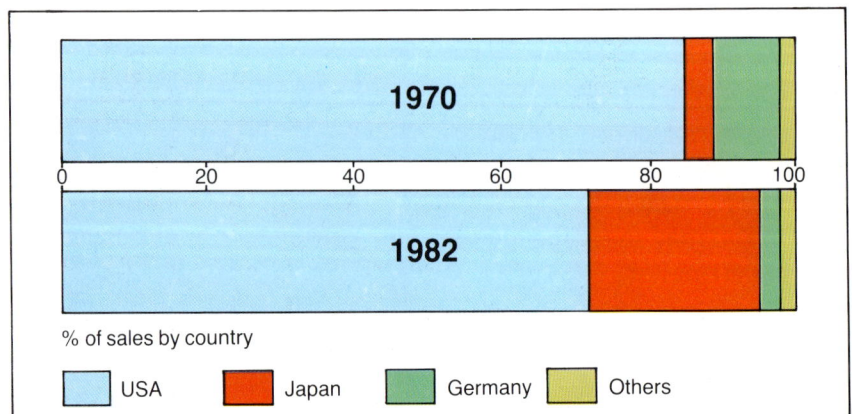

% of sales by country

USA | Japan | Germany | Others

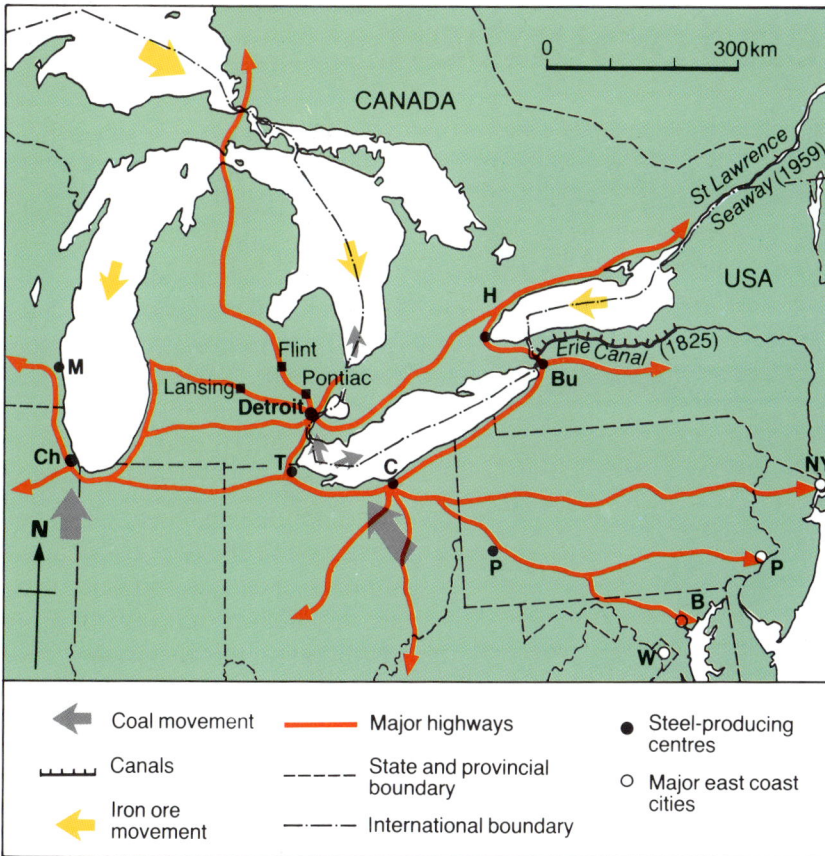

Coal movement — Major highways — ● Steel-producing centres
⊔⊔⊔ Canals — --- State and provincial boundary — ○ Major east coast cities
Iron ore movement — -·-·- International boundary

3 Detroit and the Great Lakes area. Good access to raw materials and markets helped to make Detroit the centre of America's car industry. In the 1960s, the city had over a quarter of all the car-making jobs in the USA.

1 Copy picture 3 and with the help of your atlas:
(a) Name the five lakes that make up the Great Lakes.
(b) Name the steel-producing centres.
(c) Name the main east-coast cities.

2 Look at picture 3 and read these pages again. Why did Detroit become the centre of the car industry in the USA?

3 What is a 'drive-in'? Try to suggest some advantages and disadvantages in having them.

4 Pictures 1 and 2 show recent changes that have affected the US car industry.
(a) Describe what these changes were.
(b) About 35% of Detroit's industrial workers and as many as 80% of those in towns such as Flint, Lansing and Pontiac are engaged in making cars. What may have been the effect of these changes upon them?
(c) In 1960, the city of Detroit had a population of 1 670 000. By 1980 it was 1 192 000. Try to account for this.

5 Why do you think that such small car-making firms as Buick, Cadillac and many others were unable to survive separately, while the larger, richer companies, such as General Motors, grew?

4 In a drive-in cafeteria, customers do not need to get out of their cars to be served quickly with a drink or meal.

From Frostbelt to Sunbelt

1 Decaying and derelict factories can be seen today in many of the old industrial centres of the USA.

North Americans have always been ready to get up and go in search of a better life. Over the past 200 years, they have set off by wagon train, railway, motor vehicle or aircraft to settle in other parts of North America. Many settle down and stay in the places they have moved to. Others are prepared to move many times in search of new job opportunities and a better life style. Most people have usually found these opportunities in the towns and cities, where there are jobs in the manufacturing and **service industries**.

In the past, the manufacturing region of the north-eastern states (picture 4) was the place where thousands of immigrants settled. It was also the destination for the blacks escaping from poverty in the southern states. For example, many people went to Detroit to work in the thriving car industry. As the cities grew, so did the number of service jobs, such as buying, selling, driving, repairing and cleaning.

The north-east still has half of all the manufacturing jobs in the USA. But it is today facing growing competition from the southern and western states. People are moving to these areas from the north-east in search of fresh opportunities. Some large companies have moved to the south or west, and many new ones have started there. Land is usually cheaper, taxes and wages lower, and trade unions weaker. In addition the climate is warmer and sunnier and has much

milder winters than the northern 'Frostbelt' states. So this southern region has been given the name 'Sunbelt'.

Many of America's newer, growing industries are found in the Sunbelt. They include aerospace, electronics and petrochemicals. More traditional industries, such as textiles, steel and shipbuilding, have also been attracted to the region. Cheaper supplies of oil, gas and electricity are available in the Sunbelt. Air-conditioning has also made working and living there more comfortable.

'The last one out of Michigan, turn off the lights'. How serious is this car sticker message? Certainly, the Sunbelt is growing more rapidly in population than the older manufacturing region of the north-east. Yet between 1970 and 1980 Michigan still had a small rise in population.

2 US population growth from 1800 to 1980, with the percentage of people living in rural and urban areas.

Year	Population in millions	% rural	% urban
1800	5	95	5
1820	10	94	6
1840	17	90	10
1860	31	82	18
1880	50	75	25
1900	76	64	36
1920	110	49	51
1940	131	44	56
1960	180	30	70
1980	226	27	73

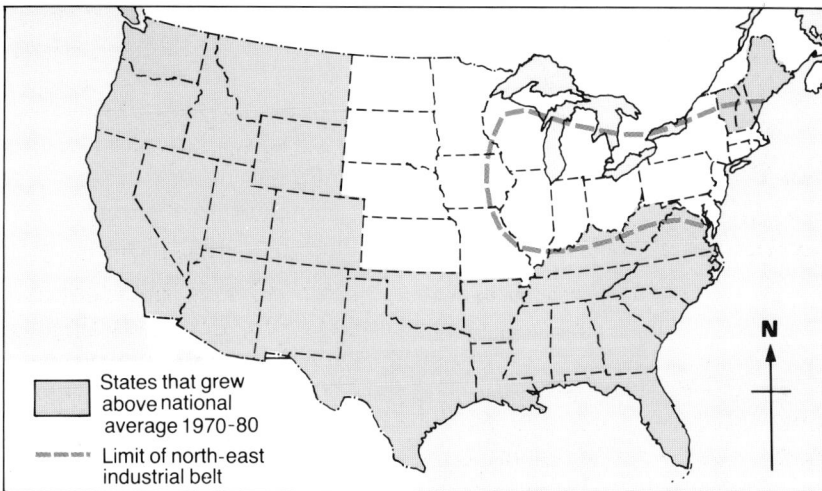

3 (above) Clean, modern factories surrounded by spacious car parks provide attractive working conditions for the rapidly growing population of the Sunbelt. In California's Silicon Valley, for example, there are scores of factories like these covering much of the Valley. Over 1 500 000 people now live there, with about 700 000 in the nearby city of San Jose, one of the USA's fastest-growing cities. (See pages 38-39.)

4 (left) States with an above-average growth in population from 1970 to 1980, and the location of the north-east industrial belt.

1 If you were about to build a factory in the USA, what might attract you to the Sunbelt?

2 Use picture 4 and your atlas for the following:
(a) On a map of the USA, shade in the states where the population grew above the national average between 1970 and 1980.
(b) Mark on the north-east industrial belt.
(c) Write down what you have noticed about the faster-growing states.
(d) Use a black pen to mark on the following cities that lost more than 10% of their population between 1970 and 1980:

Atlanta, Baltimore, Buffalo, Boston, Chicago, Cincinnati, Cleveland, Detroit, Kansas City, Louisville, Milwaukee, Minneapolis, Newark, New York City, Philadelphia, Pittsburgh, St Louis, Washington DC.

(e) Use a red pen to mark on the following cities that increased their population by more than 10% between 1970 and 1980:

Albuquerque, Austin, Charlotte, El Paso, Houston, Phoenix, San Antonio, San Diego, San Jose, Tucson.

(f) What do you notice about your map? Is this what you expected? Explain your answer.

3 Phoenix is one of the fastest-growing cities in North America. Its average temperature in July is just over 32 °C. Why do you think it is so important to have air-conditioning in homes, shops, places of work, cars and trucks?

4 Study picture 2.
(a) Draw bar graphs to show how the population of the USA grew from 1800 to 1980.
(b) Divide each bar to show the percentage of people living in rural and urban areas. Colour the rural population in green and the urban in red.
(c) Explain the changes shown on your graphs.

The Southern Dream?

'By visiting Florida you can experience our beautiful beaches, warm sunshine, lush forests and peaceful lakes. You will be able to enjoy our water sports, exciting natural and man-made attractions, championship fishing and fantastic golf and tennis.' So writes the governor of the 'Sunshine State'.

Florida is many things. It is the home of the Walt Disney World, which has 20 million visitors a year. It is the site of the Kennedy Space Center, from where the space shuttles are launched. It is famous for its beach resorts, such as Palm Beach and Miami Beach. It has ranches where cattle and thoroughbred horses are raised. In the low-lying swamps and woodlands of the Everglades there are black bears and alligators. Florida's juicy oranges and grapefruits are world-famous. There are the football games of the Miami Dolphins and motor racing at Daytona. Florida's tennis courts have produced such star players as Chris Lloyd.

Florida is best known as a holiday area. For many people it is also a good place to live after retirement, and about 17% of the state's population is over the age of 65. For others, it is a place to start a new life. Florida has a population of about ten million and welcomes, on average, a further 4000 new arrivals each week. Today, there are over 40 000 Haitians in Miami, and in 1980 about 90 000 Cubans arrived in the city. Both groups were refugees, forced to leave their homelands by poverty and politics. Almost half of Miami's population of about 350 000 now consists of people from Spanish-speaking countries. Many English-speaking whites have moved to Fort Lauderdale.

Although Florida has many attractions, it also has its problems. About 70% of all the illegal drugs that enter the USA are smuggled in through southern Florida. Drugs such as cocaine and marijuana are part of a 'business' thought to be worth up to $12 000 million a

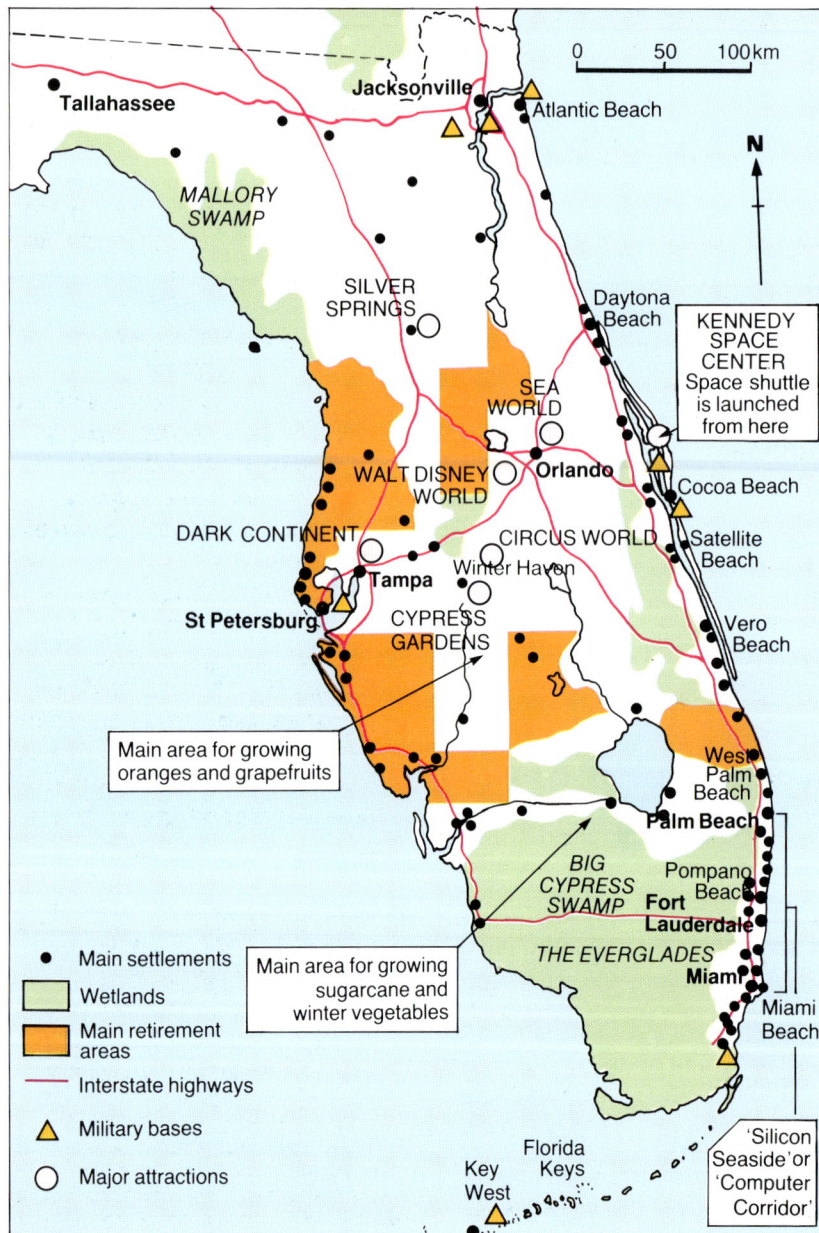

1 The main settlements, natural features and visitor attractions of Florida.

2 Walt Disney World is a huge family entertainment park near Orlando in central Florida. It offers a wide range of attractions and activities for visitors of all ages. Of special appeal to children are the cartoon characters and the thrilling rides in the Magic Kingdom.

year. In 1980, 18 people died in race riots in the black ghetto of Liberty City in Miami. Miami itself has a high crime rate. Florida law allows residents to carry handguns in their cars, and many do so.

The weather, too, can present problems. Hurricanes regularly strike the islands of the Florida Keys and other coastal areas.

They cause damage costing millions of dollars each year. In 1981, a drought brought serious water shortages to many areas. At times Florida, the 'southern dream', may seem more like a nightmare.

3 Monthly average temperatures in degrees Celsius (°C) for the cities of Chicago (Illinois) and Tampa (Florida).

Month	J	F	M	A	M	J	J	A	S	O	N	D
Temperature (°C)												
Chicago	−3	−2	2	9	13	20	23	22	19	12	4	−1
Tampa	16	17	19	22	25	27	28	28	27	24	20	17

4 These homes were wrecked by a hurricane. Hurricanes form in the Caribbean area every year and sometimes sweep north over the USA. Florida is one of the southern states that lie in their path.

1 What would attract you to Florida for a holiday, and why? What might put you off?

2 The railway reached Tampa in 1885 and Miami in 1896. How do you think this helped the early tourist industry?

3 Use the temperature figures for Chicago and Tampa to answer the questions below.
(a) On the same graph base, draw two line graphs showing the monthly temperatures in each city, Chicago in blue and Tampa in red. Draw a line across to mark freezing point.
(b) Describe the differences between the temperatures in the two cities.
(c) If you lived in Chicago, what would make Tampa an attractive place for retirement?

4 Use picture 1 to help you to answer the following:
(a) There are about 100 dots on the map, each representing a main settlement. Work out roughly what percentage of settlements are within 25 km of the coast.
(b) Which coast would you expect to attract most of the people wanting a seaside holiday? Explain your decision.
(c) Where are most of the main attractions, such as Walt Disney World? Why do you think this area was a good one to choose for these types of attraction?

5 The USA is concerned about political unrest in Central America and the Caribbean area. Cuba is a communist country. How does this help to explain the number of military bases in Florida?

Silicon Valley

1 (above) A hi-tech factory in Silicon Valley. Special clothing helps to prevent the dust particles on ordinary clothing damaging the microscopic silicon chips.

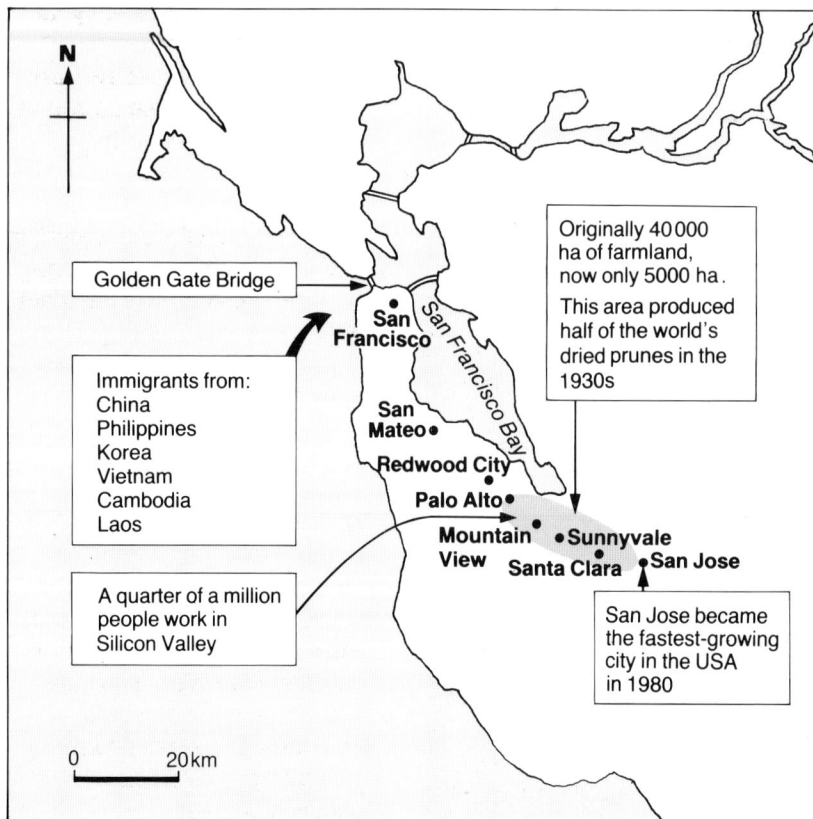

N

Golden Gate Bridge

San Francisco

San Francisco Bay

Immigrants from:
China
Philippines
Korea
Vietnam
Cambodia
Laos

San Mateo

Redwood City

Palo Alto

Mountain View

Sunnyvale

Santa Clara

San Jose

A quarter of a million people work in Silicon Valley

Originally 40 000 ha of farmland, now only 5000 ha.
This area produced half of the world's dried prunes in the 1930s

San Jose became the fastest-growing city in the USA in 1980

0   20km

2 Silicon Valley, California – a 32 km corridor of firms making microchips and many of the things that use microchips. Average incomes here are among the highest in the USA – but so too are house prices.

The farmland between Palo Alto and San Jose, in California, used to produce half of the world's dried prunes. Today, that same area is the heartland of the American electronics industry. It is known as 'Silicon Valley'. This dramatic change began in 1959, when the **silicon chip** was first produced there on a large scale and brought about a revolution in the electronics industry. It led to today's high-technology industries, popularly known as 'hi-tech'.

More than 80 firms now produce chips in Silicon Valley. Many other firms use the chips to make computers, watches, games and other electronic devices. There are also other companies which transport and sell these products. Nearby Stanford University does much of the research needed for new developments. This university is a world leader in electronics research, and its presence in this area was one of the main reasons for the growth of Silicon Valley's hi-tech industries.

For some people, a job in Silicon Valley has brought rich rewards, including high salaries, big houses and expensive cars. But there are others who are not so well paid. Many are immigrants, mostly Hispanics and Asians, who work on the assembly lines for very low wages. Few of them can afford to buy their own homes, because the cost of property keeps rising.

Because of high land prices in Silicon Valley, some firms have now moved to other parts of the USA and abroad. Apple Computer, for example, is still based in Silicon Valley but also has plants in Texas and Singapore. While National Semiconductor has also set up in Arizona and Malaysia.

There are other problems. With about a quarter of a million people travelling to and from work every day, the roads cannot cope with the number of cars, and traffic jams occur regularly. **Smog** is becoming more common. In 1981, it was found that chemicals had leaked into the local water supply. There are also strains on family life, and Santa Clara County has a higher number of divorces than marriages.

The electronics industry is a very competitive business, and new discoveries are vital if firms are to go on making money. Stealing new ideas from competitors is becoming more common and is done by both American companies and foreign rivals. For them, being first with a new product is what really counts.

3 Some of the uses for silicon chips.

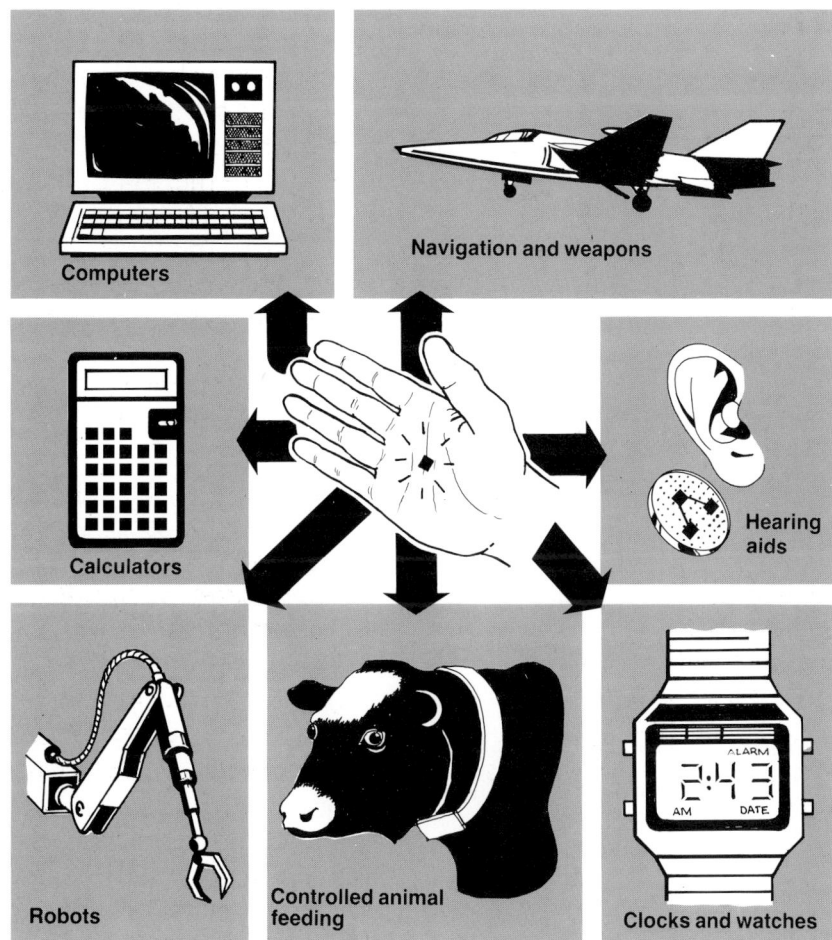

Computers

Navigation and weapons

Calculators

Hearing aids

Robots

Controlled animal feeding

Clocks and watches

1 People producing chips, making computers, selling electronic equipment and doing research are all found in Silicon Valley. What are the advantages for jobs that have something in common to be close together?

2 In 1980, about 50 000 new jobs became available in Silicon Valley, but only 12 000 new homes were built. Why was this a problem, and what effect do you think it had on house prices in the area?

3 Many people **commute** long distances to work. The average distance is over 25 km.
(a) What problems have arisen as more and more people drive to work?
(b) Why are the distances people commute likely to get even longer?
(c) Imagine that you drive to work in Silicon Valley every day. Describe how you may feel during the journey, and by the time you get home.
(d) Building new roads is very expensive. How else do you think traffic jams may be reduced?

4 Try to explain why some people in Silicon Valley have become rich, while others cannot afford to buy a house.

5 Why do think that some immigrants are willing to work for low wages? What other difficulties do they have to overcome?

6 **Project idea:** Design a wall display to show how important the silicon chip has become in our everyday lives. You may include pictures or your own drawings, or perhaps even graphics produced on your school computer.

Cities in the Sun

History was made on 21 July 1969, when Neil Armstrong became the first man to set foot on the moon. His spacecraft had blasted off from Cape Canaveral, in Florida, but the whole operation was handled by Mission Control in Houston, Texas. Here, at the Lyndon B. Johnson Space Center on the outskirts of the city, the National Aeronautics and Space Administration (NASA) has its headquarters. This has given Houston the title of 'Space City, USA'.

Hitting the headlines is not new to Houston. In 1901, oil was

1 (above) In the Rio Grande valley of south-western Texas, up to 50 000 Mexican-Americans live in 'colonias', or ghettos, of simple shacks. Only half of the homes here have piped-water, and none has proper sewerage.

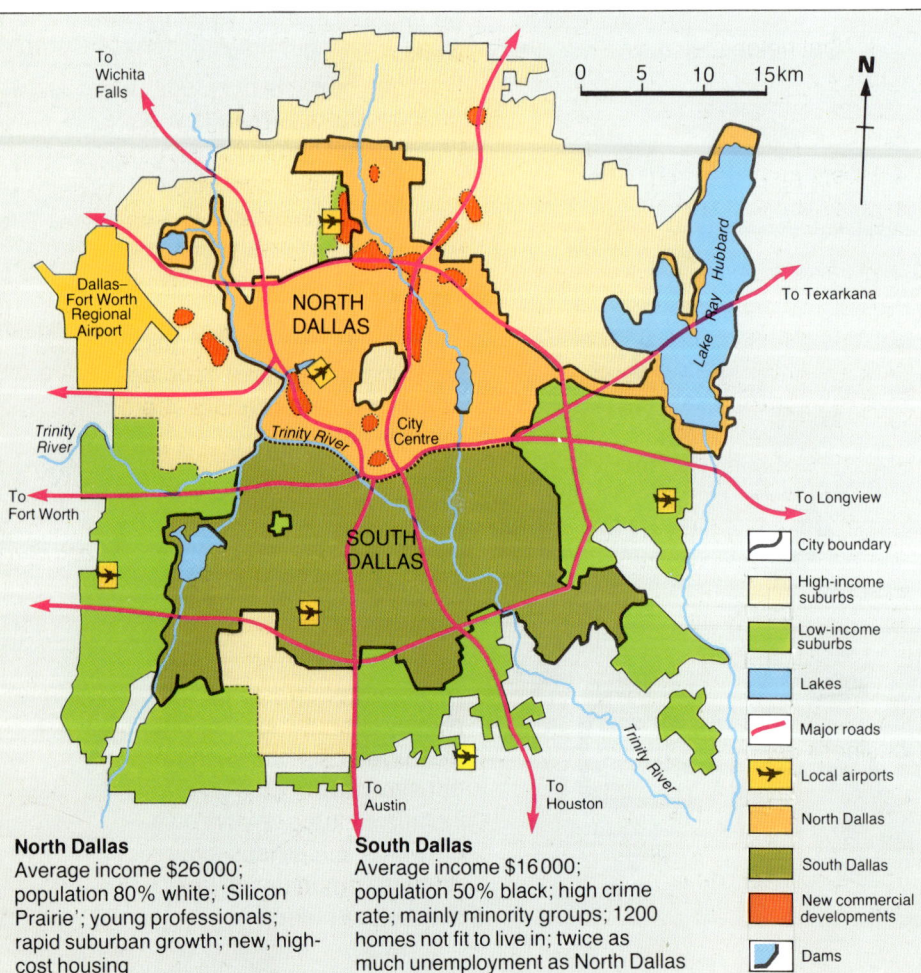

2 (left) The city and suburbs of Dallas, Texas. Dallas grew rapidly in the 1870s, when the railway arrived. As it was the end of the line for several years, it soon developed into an important trading centre. Today, American Airlines, based at Dallas–Fort Worth airport, operates flights to almost 140 North American cities.

North Dallas
Average income $26 000; population 80% white; 'Silicon Prairie'; young professionals; rapid suburban growth; new, high-cost housing

South Dallas
Average income $16 000; population 50% black; high crime rate; mainly minority groups; 1200 homes not fit to live in; twice as much unemployment as North Dallas

Legend:
- City boundary
- High-income suburbs
- Low-income suburbs
- Lakes
- Major roads
- Local airports
- North Dallas
- South Dallas
- New commercial developments
- Dams

found at nearby Spindletop, and Houston became the 'Oil Centre of the Nation'. The name of the city's National Football League team – Houston Oilers – reminds us of this importance.

Although the city centre is 80 km from the sea, the Houston Ship Channel, opened in 1914, has helped to turn Houston into a major port. It is second only to New York City in the value of trade handled by its docks.

Houston is also a rapidly growing city, both in population and size. The city itself has over 1.5 million people, with about the same number in the surrounding urban area. Its council has allowed it to grow outward without any control. So the built-up area now spreads about 60 km from west to east and 40 km from north to south.

North-west of Houston lie two other important Texan cities. Dallas and Fort Worth are so close to each other that they share what is claimed to be the world's largest airport. They are, however, very different from each other. Fort Worth represents the old Texas. It is the headquarters of the Texas cattle industry, and parts of it, such as the Stockyards, have kept the character of the 'Old West'.

Dallas, by contrast, has a city centre of modern high-rise office buildings, elegant stores and fine restaurants. It is a major international **commercial centre** as well as an important manufacturing city. Although the main Texas oilfields are some distance away, oil companies have been attracted to the city, along with banking, insurance and other businesses. One reason for this is the transport network that makes Dallas easy to reach and to travel around. Processing farm produce, designing and manufacturing clothes and, more recently, the electronics industry have provided plenty of jobs in Dallas. They have also attracted many newcomers to the city, making Dallas one of the USA's fastest growing cities.

1 Dallas has become one of the largest and richest cities in North America.
(a) What helped its early growth?
(b) What has encouraged more recent growth?
(c) List the types of work that provide employment there.

2 Look at picture 2.
(a) The 'new commercial developments' are mainly huge shopping centres or malls. In which part of Dallas are most of them found?
(b) Try to explain why most of the 'new commercial developments' are away from the city centre and close to main roads.
(c) How many local airports are there in Dallas?
(d) What does this tell you about the importance of Dallas as a business centre?

3 Dallas is a city with two very different halves. Use picture 2 to describe some of the differences.

3 With more and more people going to live in America's Sunbelt, well-planned suburbs with modern, comfortable homes are being built around such cities as Phoenix, Arizona, shown above.

4 Houston has the highest average family income of all the main North American cities (Dallas is in second place). What has helped Houston to become so important and wealthy?

5 Imagine you are the first person to step on to the moon. Describe your fears and excitement. What words might you say to Mission Control as you set foot on the surface?

6 **Project idea:** The USA has been involved in space exploration since 1926. Work in groups to make a wall display showing the different space programmes in which the USA has been involved. They include early rockets and satellites, people in space and on the moon, the space shuttle, Skylab, and, more recently, the 'Star-Wars' project.

Getting About

1 An Amtrak passenger train.

Being able to get about quickly, easily and comfortably is very important in a land as vast as North America. It was the railways that first made it possible to travel long distances in reasonable comfort. But with growing competition from road and air transport, passenger services on the railways began to lose money. As a result, many stations were closed and the number of passenger trains was cut.

In 1970 the US government stepped in to prevent further cuts. It set up an organization called Amtrak to handle all passenger services to some 500 towns and cities in 44 states. Amtrak now operates on 40 000 km of track. It has tried to win back customers by introducing new and more comfortable coaches and a service that runs on time. The choice of accommodation ranges from 'day coaches', with reclining seats, to 'roomettes', with a separate lounge, bedroom and bathroom. Many journeys may not be particularly fast, due to the poor state of the track, but they are comfortable. People are also attracted by the competitively priced fares.

The Canadian government has followed a similar course to the USA by setting up VIA Rail. This has ensured that passenger trains will continue to run in Canada.

Motorways, called expressways, freeways or interstate highways, link most parts of North America. On some motorways, called turnpikes, drivers have to pay to use the road. A maximum speed limit of 88 km/h (55 mph) is enforced by police patrols, radar and aircraft. This may make driving safer, but it also means that long journeys take more time.

Bus companies offer excellent services. They link cities, towns and villages throughout the continent and stop in what often seems to be the middle of nowhere! Two companies, Greyhound and Trailways, between them operate almost 7 000 buses. The fares are quite cheap and the buses are reasonably comfortable, but they are slow. The 1340 km journey from Chicago to New Orleans takes 25 hours by bus, but only about two hours by air.

2 A Greyhound bus. See picture 3 on page 7 for the times taken by Greyhound buses to travel between the main North American cities.

The need to get to distant places quickly has made air travel popular in North America. In the USA ten main airlines operate long-distance 'trunk lines' serving the whole country. Many more airlines run shorter regional and commuter lines. 'Air taxi' services using smaller aircraft and helicopters help people to get quickly from one side of a city to the other.

1 There are more and more cars on the roads, and airports are becoming even busier. Suggest reasons why both the US and Canadian governments wanted to keep passenger services on the railways.

2 Why do you think that a rise in oil and petrol prices in 1979 encouraged more people to travel by train?

3 List what you think are the advantages and disadvantages of travelling by car, bus, train or aircraft for (a) short distances, (b) long distances. (Think about speed, cost, comfort and so on.)

4 Picture 3 shows the four main time zones of the USA and some of the services operated by American Airlines from Dallas–Fort Worth Airport.
(a) Why do you think Dallas–Fort Worth is such a busy airport?
(b) Make a copy of the map. Where there is a '?' work out either the local time of arrival or the journey time and add to your map.
(c) How may the crossing of time zones make travel arrangements more difficult than in Britain?

(d) Why do countries such as Canada and the USA have different times in the east and west?
(e) Find out which other countries need more than one time zone.

5 Project ideas:
(a) Describe and draw pictures to show what you think it will be like in the future if people go on producing more and more cars, lorries, aircraft and so on.
(b) Oil is used to make petrol, diesel fuel and aviation fuel. What do you think will happen when oil supplies run out?

3 Air links between Dallas and other major US cities. Flying times are shown for some routes. Because North America stretches so far from east to west, there are eight different 'time zones' across its territory. Four of them are within mainland USA. So when it is 10 o'clock in New York, it is still 7 o'clock in San Francisco, as the clocks on the map show.

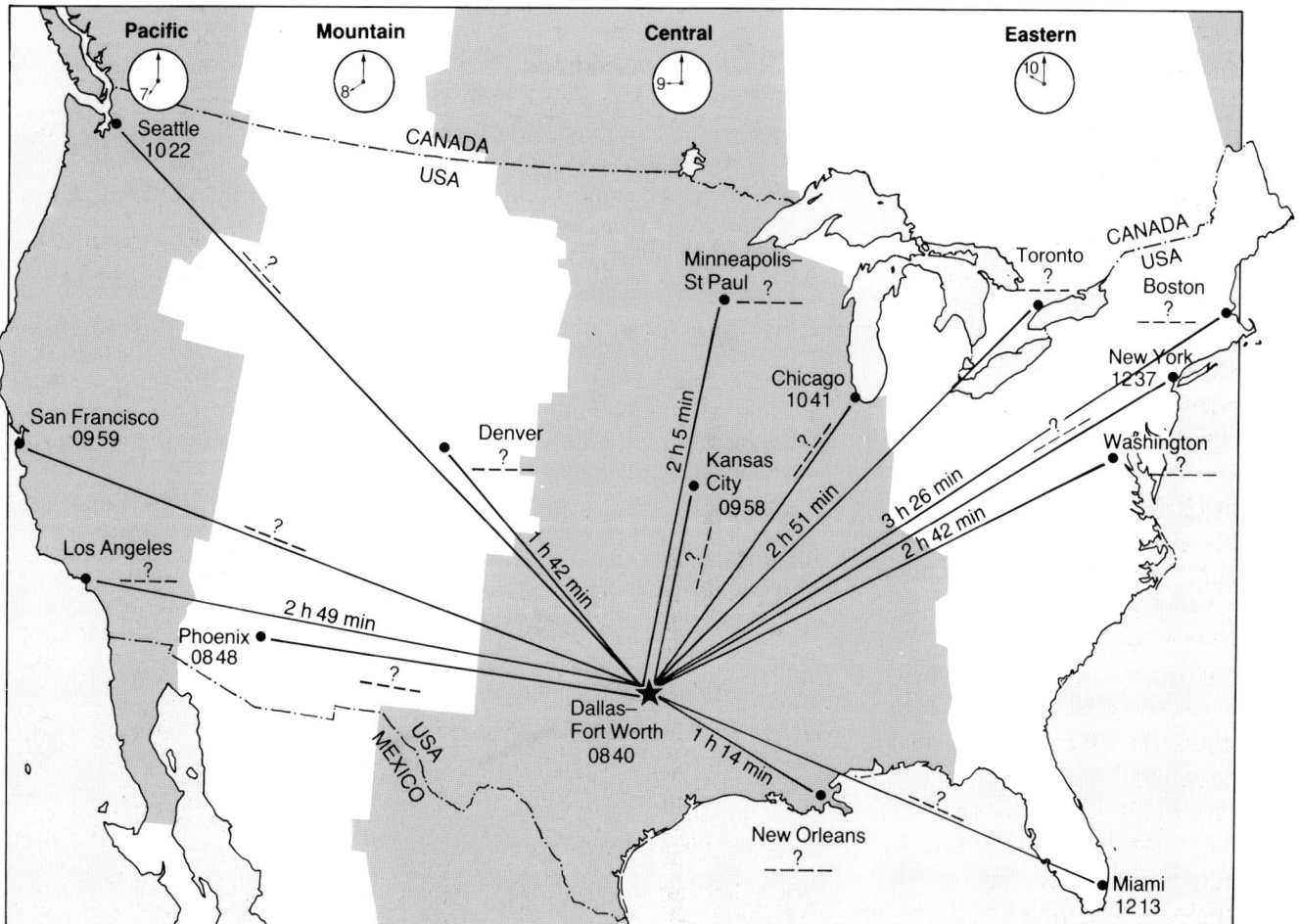

Time to Spare

Yellowstone, in the Rocky Mountains of Wyoming, became the world's first National Park in 1872. Since then the USA has continued to set aside areas of special interest to protect them from being badly used. Mountains, volcanoes, glaciers, canyons, caves, deserts, forests, coasts, lakes and swamps are all included in the 39 US National Parks. National Forests, Recreation Areas, Wilderness Parks and all kinds of State Parks also exist to keep even more land from development.

Canada was not far behind its neighbour. In 1885, Banff became Canada's first National Park. Today, there are 28 of these parks, covering about 130 000 km^2, an area almost the same size as England and Wales. Historic, Provincial and Wilderness Parks provide even more open spaces for Canadians.

Wilderness Parks are just that – large, untouched areas in which few people set foot. Some can only be reached by using 'float-planes' that can land on lakes, or by 'back-packing' on foot from the nearest road or track.

Although the Wilderness Parks may continue to be little used, other parks have created considerable growth in the tourist industry in some areas. Examples are Yellowstone and the Grand Canyon. The popularity of such places may in the future damage those special environments that the National Parks were intended to preserve.

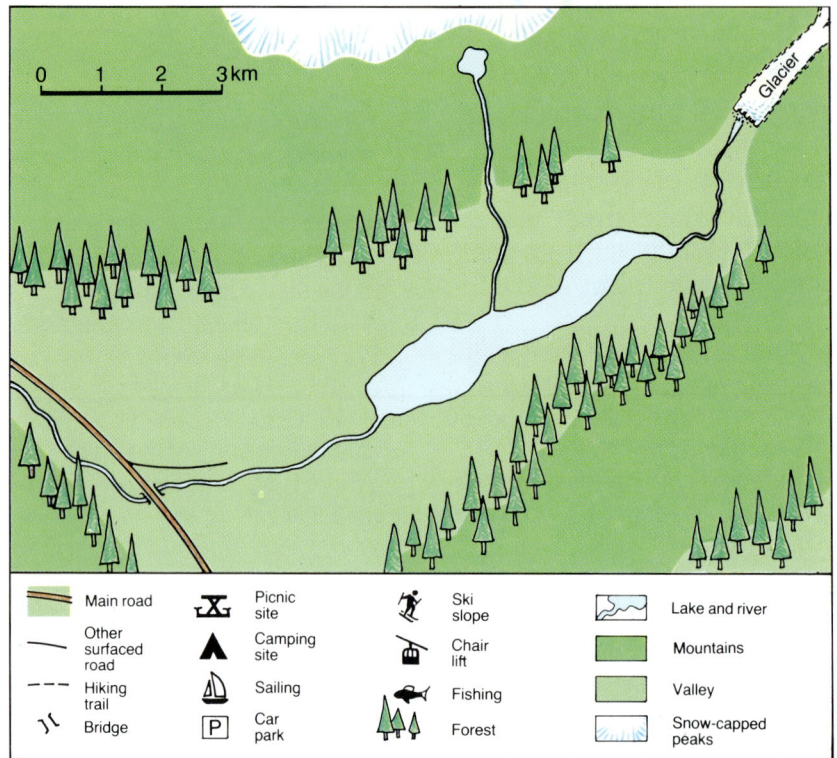

Key:
- Main road
- Other surfaced road
- Hiking trail
- Bridge
- Picnic site
- Camping site
- Sailing
- Car park
- Ski slope
- Chair lift
- Fishing
- Forest
- Lake and river
- Mountains
- Valley
- Snow-capped peaks

1 Look at the information on Banff National Park on page 45.
(a) Why do you need to be careful about animals?
(b) Suggest why you should never go into wilderness areas alone.
(c) Why do you think it is a good idea to 'register out' and 'in' when you are attempting 'hazardous activities'?
(d) Why should people 'pack out litter'?
(e) What could be the dangers of lighting fires?
(f) Do you think that hunting is allowed in the park? Explain your answer.
(g) Do you think it is right to make motor vehicles keep to the public roads only? Give your reasons.

2 All the parks in North America are intended to give people the chance of enjoying outdoor leisure pursuits. How may the growing popularity of some parks actually result in damage to them?

3 The picture above shows an imaginary area that could be developed in a Provincial Park.
(a) Draw your own larger version of the map and give an approximate scale for it. You may add your own names for mountains, lakes and other features.
(b) Plan out how you would use this area for both summer and winter activities. Use the ideas provided in the key and any of your own.
(c) Write a short guide for people who may wish to use the park. Describe its attractions, suggest how long some of the walks would take, and mention any dangers and anything else you think is important.

Banff National Park

Parks Canada
Parcs Canada

A SPECIAL PLACE

You have crossed the frontier to a very special place — one of Canada's national parks. It has been set aside for you and generations yet to come.

National parks are basically wilderness preserves maintained by Parks Canada for the benefit, enjoyment and education of all Canadians. To visitors from other lands, we extend a welcome to our special heritage.

Before you venture farther there are a few things you should know that will make your visit pleasant and safe.

Animals in this park may appear tame but they are wild and can be dangerous. For your protection and for theirs, it is unlawful to entice, touch or feed wildlife in a national park. Respect their wild and free nature — observe but don't intrude. For specific information about bears, consult the *"You are in Bear Country"* folder available at information centres and park gateways. Since many animals tend to congregate along roadways, drive attentively and at somewhat reduced speeds.

Safety is your own personal responsibility. Natural hazards exist in all areas of the park and caution must be exercised during your visit to Banff National Park. Travel in wilderness areas should be done with a companion. He or she could save your life. Proper footwear and clothing are survival "musts".

Camping is allowed in designated areas only. If all campgrounds are filled, park personnel and signs will help direct you to an overflow camping area.

Backcountry activities involving an overnight stay require a park use permit. This mandatory permit is available at park warden offices and information centres along with information about trails and campsites. You may voluntarily register out for any activities considered hazardous. You must, however, register back in.

Pack out litter and refuse with you from trails and campsites where no garbage disposal facilities exist. Litter bags are available from information centres and park warden offices.

Fires may be lit only in fireplaces provided.

Fishing is permitted in most park waters. Anglers must first obtain a national parks fishing permit and a copy of the fishing regulations.

Firearms must be sealed at gun sealing stations at park entrances.

Motor vehicles including automobiles, trucks, motor bikes and all-terrain vehicles are restricted to use on public roads only. Oversnow vehicles may be used on designated trails only.

Pets must be leashed at all times while in Banff National Park. Pets can provoke confrontation with wildlife and it may be hazardous to take them with you on park trails.

A variety of interpretive programs, including walks and evening presentations, are provided by park interpreters. They will help you appreciate Banff National Park, both in summer and winter. For more information ask for an interpretive program schedule at any park information centre.

Lake Louise

Athabaska Glacier

The Last Frontier

The Northwest Territories and Yukon make up nearly 40% of Canada's area. But only 0.2% of Canada's population live there. Many are Indians living in the forested areas and Eskimos living further north in the tundra. The rest are mostly people working for mining firms. With air temperatures as low as −80 °C, living and working in the far north is difficult and unpleasant.

Although Canada covers about 9.8 million km² of land, most of its 23 million people live close to the US border in the south. This is hardly surprising, as the climate is warmer here, the land is easier to farm and communications are good. Half of Canada's population is, in fact, found along the St Lawrence Valley and in south-western Ontario.

The search for wealth in the cold northern lands has been going on for 100 years. In the 1890s, there was the Klondike gold rush. In the 1960s, there was the discovery of Alaskan oil. The minerals known to exist in the wilderness stretching from Alaska to Labrador include uranium, nickel, silver, gold, zinc, cobalt, silica, lead and asbestos. Mining has begun in many isolated places.

In northern Quebec, **hydroelectric power** has been generated since 1979. By the year 2000 the hydroelectric scheme on the La Grande River will be producing 13 700 MW. This is more than the total power produced by Britain's six largest power stations together.

All this activity has brought new jobs, new industries and thousands of 'outsiders' to the northlands. It has also brought great changes to the ways of life of the native peoples. Many traditional skills are in danger of being lost. Some young people show more interest in cars and TV than in hunting and fishing. In some village schools, however, traditional dances and sledge

1 The native peoples of the Arctic lands.

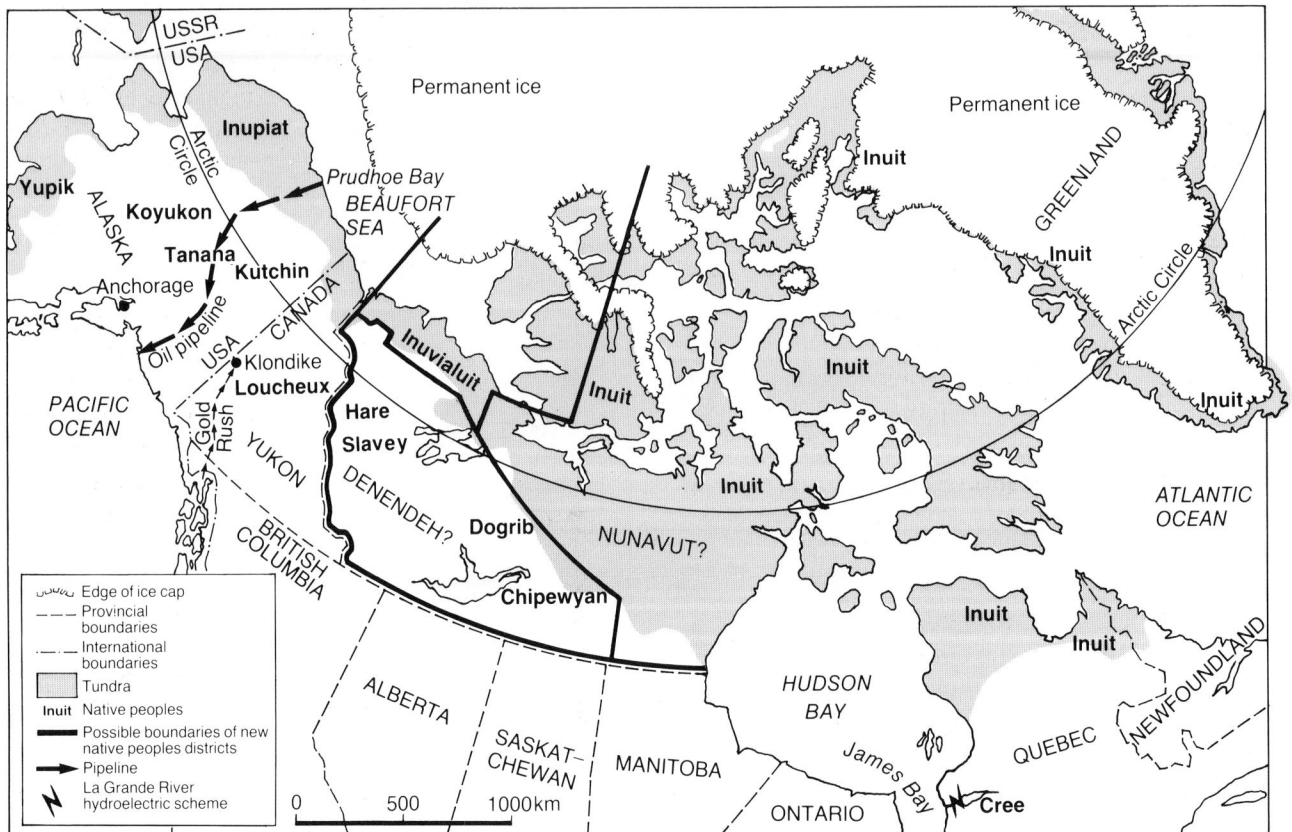

1 The native peoples of the Arctic lands.

2 The Inuit settlement of Frobisher Bay, the main town on Baffin Island. Among the buildings are shacks used by seal-catchers.

making are taught alongside computing.

Two important questions have to be answered. Who owns the land and the minerals? And what are the rights of the native peoples to have a say in the future of their homelands?

In 1971 the US government gave $1000 million and 18 million ha of land to the 85 000 native people of Alaska. Without this agreement, the future of Alaskan oil operations would have been uncertain. In 1975 the Canadian government made a similar deal with the Cree Indians and Inuits of northern Quebec. As a result, work could be started on the La Grande River hydroelectric scheme.

In the Northwest Territories, both the Indian and Inuit peoples have voted to divide the land between them. They want greater control of their own lands, which would be called Denendeh and Nunavut. Both names mean Our Land.

Chief Tommy Charlie
A Loucheux Indian who has spent all his life in an isolated village north of the Arctic Circle in the Yukon.

Methusalah Otak
A young Inuit who has not learned the traditional crafts and skills. When he leaves school he will probably be unemployed.

Sharon Williams
A recently qualified engineer from Ottawa. Free food, housing and recreation will let her save most of the $700 a week she can earn.

1 Why have most Canadian settlers chosen to live in the southern parts of their country?

2 Fur traders from the Hudson's Bay Company first made contact with the Inuit 300 years ago. This had little effect on the Inuit lifestyle. Why do you think that contact with 'outsiders' since the 1950s has had so much more effect?

3 Why is there so much interest in the northlands at present?

4 Why do you think that the native peoples want to sort out who owns the land and to have a greater say in the future of their homelands?

5 Look at the people on the left.
(a) Write down how you think each person would feel about a new mining operation in the northlands.
(b) Imagine you are one of the people shown. Explain in more detail how a new mining operation might affect you. What opportunities might it provide? Would you see it as a good or bad thing – or perhaps a bit of both? How would it affect your future?

6 (a) Suggest some reasons why the Canadian government has generally been slow to make decisions about the land claims of native peoples in the north.
(b) Why have some decisions been made more quickly?

7 **Project idea:** Find out more about the Alaskan pipeline or the La Grande hydroelectric scheme. Why were these necessary? How difficult was their construction? What is it like to work on such projects? How have they changed the lives of people living in the area?

Glossary

Assembly line: A method of manufacturing in which a product, such as a motor car, is put together piece by piece as it moves past a series of workers. Each worker has his or her own separate task in the operation.

Civil war: A war fought between people who are part of the same nation.

Colony: A country or region taken over, settled and governed by another nation. The government of a colony is partly controlled from the home country.

Commercial centre: A place that carries on a large amount of trade and as a result has become wealthy.

Commute: To travel regularly to and from a place of work. People who do this are called commuters.

Dysentery: An illness usually caused by drinking water containing sewage.

Environment: Your surroundings at any particular time, such as where you live or work.

Ethnic group: A group of people who share the same origins, beliefs, traditions and cultures.

Ghetto: Originally an area in European cities where Jews were forced to live. The word is now used to describe a densely populated district in a city where one particular group or nationality is concentrated. It is often a poor-quality area.

Hispanic: A person who speaks Spanish as his or her main language.

Hydroelectric power (HEP): Electricity made by using the energy of running water.

Immigrant: A person who settles in a country where he or she was not born. The movement of immigrants into a country is called immigration.

Industrial corporation: A big company which produces the goods or services we use in everyday life. The largest corporations are often made up of a number of smaller companies called subsidiaries.

Inputs: The things that are put in or added to something to make it better. In farming they include money, people, machines, fertilizers and pesticides.

Intensive: A type of farming with many *inputs*, usually using a small area of land to produce large *yields*.

Irrigation: The supplying of water by canals, reservoirs and other means to naturally dry areas so that crops can be grown there.

Minority group: A group of people who are fewer in number than the main group(s). In North America, *Hispanics*, Asians, blacks and native Indians are minority groups.

Multi-cultural: Made up of the cultures of many nations.

New World: North, Central and South America, so called because their existence was not generally known until the voyages made by Europeans from 1492 onwards.

Nomadic: Describes the way of life of people who are continually moving around. Some nomadic peoples move with herds of animals in search of pasture.

Persecution: Being badly treated or even killed for one's beliefs.

Pioneer: Someone who is among the first to achieve something new. In North American history, the pioneers were the first settlers to travel to the west in the 1800s.

Plantation: A large estate used for growing crops for sale. In the southern states of the USA, the main crops were cotton, sugar, rice, tobacco and indigo.

Racial discrimination: Treating people unfairly because of their racial origin.

Relief: The varying height of the land formed by mountains, hills, valleys and plains.

Reservation: An area of land set aside for people to live in when their original lands are taken over by other people and used for other purposes.

Rural area: A region that is mainly countryside.

Seasonal field labour: People who work on farms at times when there is a lot of work to do, such as harvest time.

Service industries: Businesses that provide a service, such as shops and transport. People in service jobs do not make goods for sale.

Silicon chip: A small piece of silicon about the size of a finger nail which contains many tiny electrical circuits. It is used to control a computer.

Smog: A combination of smoke and fog. It is most common in towns and cities, where car exhausts and fumes from factories are more concentrated.

Soil erosion: The removal of soil (especially top soil) by wind, running water or moving ice.

Standardized parts: Parts made to the same size and shape and from the same materials.

Subsistence farmer: A farmer who produces only enough food for himself and his own family.

Tipi: A conical-shaped Indian home made from a framework of poles covered with bark or animal hides. It is sometimes wrongly called a wigwam, which has a rounded top and is covered with bark or mats, not hides.

Totem pole: A carved and often painted tall wooden pole. It usually tells a story or legend and includes the family or clan emblem. The emblem, or totem, is often an animal, such as a bear, frog or eagle.

Tundra: A region of cold, treeless plains in northern Europe, Asia and North America. Mosses, lichens and some flowering plants grow there during the short summers.

Urban area: A densely built-up area, such as a city or town.

Yield: The amount of produce that comes from farming, including crops and animal products. It is usually measured as an amount per hectare.

CENTRAL REGIONAL SCHOOL SERVICE